OUTDOOR ADVENTURES:
EQUIPPED TO LIVE IN A DANGEROUS WORLD

A FATHER'S
FIELD GUIDE
TO SUCCESS
IN CHRISTIAN
LIVING

ROBIN J. WOOD, SR.

WESTBOW
PRESS®
A DIVISION OF THOMAS NELSON
& ZONDERVAN

WestBow Press books may be ordered through booksellers or by contacting:

WestBow Press
A Division of Thomas Nelson & Zondervan
1663 Liberty Drive
Bloomington, IN 47403
www.westbowpress.com
1 (866) 928-1240

Because of the dynamic nature of the Internet, any web addresses or links contained in this book may have changed since publication and may no longer be valid. The views expressed in this work are solely those of the author and do not necessarily reflect the views of the publisher, and the publisher hereby disclaims any responsibility for them.

Any people depicted in stock imagery provided by Thinkstock are models, and such images are being used for illustrative purposes only.
Certain stock imagery © Thinkstock.

ISBN: 978-1-5127-4541-2 (sc)

Library of Congress Control Number: 2016909236

Print information available on the last page.

WestBow Press rev. date: 06/30/2016

This book is lovingly dedicated to my wife, Jackie, who has devoted her life to Christ, to me, and to our children.

CONTENTS

INTRODUCTION

"When you can't see where you're going, you have to operate on principle." A good friend once said these words. We were discussing some very difficult business decisions. Pilots know this. They depend on their instrumentation, especially when flying in the fog and in the dark. In my view, feelings are often untrustworthy, especially for men. My apologies to you strong, sensitive types. The point is that in tough situations, if we operate on emotion, we might fly into a mountain. The Bible supports this idea in II Corinthians 5:7: "For we walk by faith and not by sight" (KJV).

What is the principle my friend was talking about? The principle is decision-making from a biblical worldview. A biblical worldview is applying God's perspective to every area of your life.

John Payne says, "Our worldview is how we describe the end result of being shaped by our social, physical and spiritual environment."

This should give you some hint as to where we're headed with these writings. Yes, I'm going to write another book for men. (Certainly there aren't enough of them.) This text is also relevant for women; however, it is primarily written to focus on the needs of men.

At the time of this writing, my son, Robin Jr., was seventeen years old. I wanted to leave him a special legacy. I did this for my twenty-four-year-old daughter, Lindsay, at about the same age. She has turned out to be absolutely flawless in every way, and, if you believe that, I have a bridge in Brooklyn to sell you. I wrote seven letters on seven principles that I thought would help guide her through this maze called life. It took about a year of Sundays to accomplish this. I bound the letters in leather, and I'm certain that she'll read them, someday. She is doing just great, and she has been through them. These letters also ended up in one of the larger churches in town, becoming the curriculum for the advanced new believer's class, and have been taught in many other venues.

My intention is to change the presentation a bit this time, though. I will attempt a different format than I did for Lindsay's letters. I want to write to Robin using some of our hunting and fishing adventures. This way, if you don't like the things that I really want to say, maybe you will enjoy our incredible adventures. We've hunted trophy black bear together. Hopefully, I'll also get to stories about exotic North American fishing adventures, trout as big as salmon, and dangerous wild boar hunts. This will allow me to impart some valuable information. There may even be pictures to substantiate some of the results of our adventures. It will be written in the oral tradition that many cultures have used to pass down important information.

What kind of information will be imparted? I will share practical ideas and principles that have acted like guidance instrumentation for me through nearly forty years of walking faithfully with Christ. I said *faithfully* walking with Christ, not *flawlessly* walking with Christ. The letters are to my son, and he knows that I haven't always behaved perfectly. I won't be able to disguise these concepts with religious impracticalities. It's called something else in the streets.

I will now begin to speak in first person as if I were talking to my son, Robin, because that's what I'll be doing.

Robin, I want to talk to you about a few things that I've learned the hard way. I need to talk about truth, biblical truth. There are a lot of folks out there masquerading as Christians who don't know what *essential Christian doctrine* is. By the way, *doctrine* is defined as "something taught as the principles or creed of a religion." Though I hate the term *religion*, it will help you to understand the idea.

I have a relationship with a living God, not a religion. Doctrine actually affects practical decision-making. Practical decision-making affects life's results. The results of bad decisions are, however, the same if you're educated or not. They're called unintended consequences. Theology is derived from the word *theos*, or God. Theology is the study of God.

There are also some Christians who have a theology that is a hybrid. These believers are like the golden trout and rainbow trout hybrids that we catch at eight to ten thousand feet above sea level. By the way, I won't be naming names of aberrant Christian groups. There are ministries developed for this purpose. I will be giving guidelines that will make false doctrine apparent. A working knowledge of God's Word will also help you to see if certain beliefs fit into the filter of "all Scripture" or "the whole counsel of God." My major purpose is to give you the tools to measure your own flight patterns.

I want to talk about *the Bible*, God's Word. It has a unique history and structure. It speaks to all types of complex issues that we face in life.

PRAYER

How do we pray? What I mean is, how do we pray to receive answers? How do we pray in good times and in desperate times? You have seen your mom and me dodge the bullet more than once. It takes miraculous intervention and a deep personal relationship with the Lord to achieve consistent results. For example, King David of Israel was a man's man. He was a warrior. The Psalms reveal his true, private, inner self. He wrote of the soft underbelly of his deepest fears, hopes, anger, and other human emotions. The Psalms were his prayers, and his life demonstrated the miraculous results of a man of prayer.

SPIRITUAL WARFARE

Satan is real, and so is our flesh or fallen nature. The world's system of thought is also real. In the Bible, it is referred to as "the World." We will discuss how to take on any of these and win. How do we overcome our own destructive human desires? How do we gain victory over a cultural worldview that isn't based upon biblical principles? I'm not just talking about material stuff. I'm talking about spiritual weaponry. Please forgive me, but you don't face a charging 560-pound black bear with anything but the best and highest-caliber firearm. You know; you were there with me. God's armament is higher in quality and effectiveness than a handmade European double rifle to take down a charging, dangerous game animal.

THE CHURCH

What is the church? What is its history? What is the church designed to do? What is it not designed to do? Unrealistic expectations can bring disappointment.

STEWARDSHIP

What are spiritual gifts? How do we discover our own? How do we use them? What about vocational gifts? I'm just a business guy who believes that God has given us mentors, resources, and tools to help us be successful in ministry and in the marketplace. There is the way money, budgeting, and time management really do work. Then there is the way we think that it works. You know many of our coaches personally. They have highly successful, functioning ministries, marriages, and businesses. Rob, I'm talking about practical theology, not religious gobbledygook.

Son, I think I have been looking forward most of all to retelling the stories. Some go all the way back to Seattle, Washington, when you fought native coastal cutthroat trout in Standard on a fly rod while riding in a baby pack attached to my back. You called them "ish." There are too many wild adventures to recount them all. They include the trophy black bear that you shot with a .45-70, small game and upland game hunting where you demonstrated your excellence in marksmanship, and fishing adventures too numerous to write about in one set of letters. Three journals spanning over eighteen years are filled with the adventures and the photos. In the spirit of gentlemen sportsmen of the nineteenth and twentieth centuries, I hope to tell the story of failing our way to success. Let's make some sense of it together, and, by the way, it ain't over yet! Let's have at it.

Love, Dad

THE GRAND SLAM

> "They devoted themselves to the Apostles' teaching and to fellowship, to the breaking of bread and prayer." (Acts 2:42 KJV)

May 28, 2007
Dear Robin,

I'm not sure what gets into me. I get this idea in my head to target a certain species of fish or mammal, and I don't rest until I get it done. You have seen it in action your whole life. I'm the same way with guns, fishing gear, collectibles, or even executing a particular work of art. The list goes on. It gives me a reason to get up in the morning.

The Lord indulges me in this. He knows how I'm wired. He had a little bit to do with it. Most of these talks will be about an adventure. This just happens to be one of them.

The focus of this trip was a Sierra grand slam here in northern Central California. As you know, the grand slam is catching a rainbow trout, brown trout, brook trout, and a golden trout on a single trip.

For an ichthyologist (that's Greek for "fish expert"), it can get a bit complicated. Seeing that I am not one of them, it should be simpler.

My best guess is that there are between thirty and forty salmonoids in North America. In laymen's terms, salmonoids are fish in the trout and salmon family. One of my lifetime goals is to catch and mount a trophy-sized fish of each species and put it on the wall. I'm about halfway to catching them, but I'd better hurry up. I'm running out of time.

The adipose fin on their back, located just before the tail fin, is what primarily distinguishes salmonoids. It looks like a small appendage that has little or no use other than to let us know that it's a salmonoid.

Trout, salmon, and char fall into this category of fish. They have been my primary quest for over forty-five years of angling. I may go into further detail on this.

These four species are rarely, if ever, found in the same place. This is one reason that the grand slam is such an achievement. The golden trout (*Salmo gairdneri*) is native to California and is our state fish. Goldens live only above eight thousand feet of elevation. They live in the most secretive and remote places. This is why most trout anglers have never caught one. They are a small but beautiful strain of true wild and native trout. A golden trout approaching twelve inches is a true trophy. They are known for their brilliant colors. In their spawning colors, a male golden trout will have a bright red stripe running down its side with brilliant blue horizontal slashes stationed horizontally over them. They can have blood-red bellies and gill plates. Large dark spots that start on the rear fin begin to grow smaller and sparser as they cover the back and approach the head. Their spots are a stark contrast to the other coloration, which includes a cream-colored base coat that is splashed with primary yellow on the majority of the fish's body and fins. The lower fins are orange and yellow. The fins are finished off with a cream-colored, bright lower tip. I'll try not to wax too romantically about any of the fish that we'll be discussing and try to get right to the story in the future … maybe. They fight well and can be acrobatic like rainbows. They are true high-mountain exotics; the fine jewelry of the Sierras.

Brown trout, or as they are affectionately called by some, German Browns, are just that. They were transplanted to the United States from Germany in the 1800s. They can grow to massive sizes of up to thirty or forty pounds. In the regions that I fish for them, a fish over twenty inches is a genuine trophy. They're the bulldogs of the trout world. They live in the deeper, darker regions of the streams and lakes, and they are primarily nocturnal. Browns are voracious feeders, and they dominate deep holes, undercuts, and long stretches of slow water. They are light brown with darker brown spots; however, some have yellowish circles around their spots. Their bellies can be white, beige, or golden yellow. The intensity of colors varies in brown trout. Like all trout, the males "color up" during spawning season and grow dramatic, hooked lower jaws called *kypes*, which are used as weapons to ward off other would-be suitors during mating.

A brook trout, also called a speckled trout, is not a true trout at all. It is a char. Char differ from trout in that they have a slightly different arrangement of teeth than trout. Their spots are white on dark, versus dark on white. Char, generally, do not mate with trout. They do crossbreed with other char species, but not with trout. As we progress in this story and in the significance of my points, the word *generally* will take on new meaning.

Eastern brook trout are the species that I cut my teeth on. I fished for them in the small brooks of upstate New York where I was raised. A fifteen-incher was considered a trophy. I've caught a few of that size back east, but nothing over thirteen inches in California. They are spectacularly colored when in full spawn. The back is olive with a lighter green body. This background of green fading to yellow is also interspersed with vivid sky-blue speckles and hot-pink dots in the center of the blue speckles. The bellies can be brilliantly bright red or orange. They are great table fare, having bright orange meat most of the time. Brookies fight fabulously and can be in almost any area of the stream. Brook trout are not native to California. They were transplanted from the East Coast.

Rainbow trout are the most common to trout anglers. "Bows" are known for their fight and for leaping multiple times during the battle. Rainbows can grow to huge sizes of thirty pounds or more in the right environments, primarily lakes. A sea-run rainbow trout is called a *steelhead*. It's born in the stream or river, migrates to the ocean for a season, and returns to its place of birth to spawn. Not all rainbow trout are steelhead. Unlike the salmon, they don't die when they return to their birthplace for the first time. A "steelie" can perform this cycle of fresh to salt water several times. Steelhead are not naturally found in streams that do not freely flow to the sea. There are no steelhead in the Sierras, but I felt that it was important to discuss this species because people often ask about them.

A rainbow trout characteristically has a white or silver body and a green back with dark spots that generally run down the side of the body. The vertical lateral line can display anywhere from faint pink to bright red. Red can also adorn the gill plates. A wild rainbow is distinguished by having blue horizontal parr marks in their immature state. By the way, a golden trout will keep parr marks through maturity. A wild trout of any species will not have rubbed lower fins that have been worn by concrete tanks where they were reared. Planter fish, as they are known, are bred so that the general public can have the experience of catching trout in more accessible locations than these wild fish.

You already know a lot of this, but for the sake of our listening audience, I thought that I'd pontificate on trout biology.

Everything changes when you start to go up the mountain and over the pass. The terrain changes, and so do the smells. The flora and fauna change, and you change too. From sea level to around two thousand feet, the land goes from the flat and fertile farmland here in town to foothills. Rolling hills with oaks and dry grass in the summer are a good place to see ground squirrels, various hawks, and, if you're lucky, a coyote or two. I'm not sure how to say this politely, but you know how I feel about coyotes. We used to have California valley quail and wild ring-necked pheasants in abundance before the coyotes killed them off. Some people also attribute the losses to poisoning and to human encroachment.

If it's early enough in the morning, and it usually is pretty early when we trout fish, you might see a family of skunks. In the spring or fall, wild turkeys are also pretty common at these elevations. Wild turkeys have made an incredible comeback from near extinction in California. Buzzards and various species of hawks are also a sure sign that you are in the foothills. You see lots of them.

As you hit about two thousand to three thousand feet, there is a wonderful odor change. It is the pines. On this particular adventure where we targeted our first grand slam, your mom and sister were with us. I promised them a free weekend at the Walton Lodge, which you and I would use as base camp. I mentioned the smells and opened the window as I always do, regardless of the temperature outside. We breathed in the pine and felt a certain cleansing. As we decompressed mentally, the chill in the air gently washed our minds from the intensities of life. It's one of the only places that I feel fully at home and comfortable in my skin. I'd live up there permanently, but I've always felt that the "nasty habits" that you children and your mother have take precedence. They are the nasty habits of food, clothing, and shelter. I've seen others take the plunge before they could afford the potential struggles of country living. These rural areas have less-predictable economies than in urban regions. Besides that, I have enjoyed the game of business that takes place in the flatland … sometimes.

There are lots of rivers and streams up there—and some pretty good fishing if you know where to go and what you're doing. It's also common to see deer, gray squirrels, and stellar jays—and there's lots of other stuff up there that bites back. You and I know this because we hunt for these shy carnivores. You have a rug in your bedroom from a trophy North American black bear that you shot to prove it.

Something dramatic happens at eight to ten thousand feet. The pines become sparser, and deep canyons and huge rock formations reveal the backside of Yosemite. El Capitan and all the other beauties of the high Sierra Nevada mountain range are just over the other side. The air gets mighty thin and you can begin to feel it. As we get out to take a break and have our photo ops, the thin air is obvious when you try to run or get up too quickly.

We get to the top, and there's a big green sign that says, "Elevation 9624 ft." We are in golden trout country.

This is *our* grand slam, not my grand slam. The year is 1999, and you are nine years old. I had discovered a small brook that contained golden trout four years earlier. There were heavy rains in '95 and some of the higher elevation lakes that contained goldens flooded and spilled these jewels into more accessible lakes and streams. You may notice that I'm being a bit vague, not naming specific locations. This is for obvious reasons.

We talked your mom and sister into driving into one of these spots, and it wasn't awful long before we had caught and photographed Salmo Gardneri, the golden trout. We each caught them that day, but this was your first golden trout. It was eight and one half inches of high mountain splendor. These little gems hit like thunder and fought their hearts out.

Now it's game on. Back to the road and on to Bridesville.

I love Bridesville. I love everything about Bridesville. I love Sam's Sporting Goods. It's one of the few places that give you the straight skinny on fishing conditions when you call ahead. They're building relationships, not just selling tackle and food to starry-eyed tourists who have visions of ten-pound trout caught on a fly rod. They have plenty of absolutely everything you need at Sam's.

I love the high-mountain desert of Bridesville that reminds me so much of the Nevada I adore, and streams that run through meadows that can hold monster trout. There is the smell of sage everywhere. Spotting a deer, blue grouse, snowshoe hare, or rattlesnake is a definite possibility up there. The vistas are breathtaking as you look over the terrain and the full spectrum of colors created by flora and lichen. Snow in the higher elevations is a year-round accessory.

I love everything about Bridesville, except for the gas stations. When I questioned the outrageous price of the gas at one of the two local stations, the owner informed me that I could always walk. So I went to the other gas station in town. I was going to show that guy. The only problem was that he owned that one also, and the price was the same. I love everything about Bridesville except for the gas stations.

We got the girls all settled in and sitting by the spa, and I suppose that we ate, though I don't usually much feel like it at that point. It was off to Darren's Ponds for brook trout. We call them Darren's Ponds because I was with Harry and his son, Darren, when Darren discovered them on a previous trip. I'm sure that it wasn't really Darren who discovered them. It was probably Fremont, or Columbus, or Amerigo Vespucci, or somebody else, but as far as I'm concerned, Darren discovered them. I actually know their name, but I can't bring myself to say it out loud.

The ponds are a group of about twenty very shallow ponds connected by channels fed by underground springs, so they're very cold. This is perfect habitat for brook trout. Brookies love cold water up to 54 degrees and are the first to die off in a drought or heat spell. Goldens like it cold and flowing. Browns thrive in warm or cold water, and rainbow trout thrive somewhere in between. Though the ponds are shallow, the channels can be quite deep at Darren's Ponds, even over your head.

The combination of all these factors can lead to some pretty great fishing, especially at sunrise or dusk. The channels are good in the day, and the ponds light up with hungry trout peppering the surface with grabs of insect hatches at dusk. Plump brook trout lay in wait next to scattered clumps of grass, poised to ambush baitfish or our spinner or hand-tied flies.

And by the way, yes, I spin fish. I also fly-fish and practice catch-and-release as well as catch-and-eat at times. I joke with my catch-and-release "fly-fishing only" friends that, "I'm not that great with a fly rod. I'm just a world record holder on a fly rod." It's strange, but true. That's a different tale for a different time, though. I do enjoy fly-fishing more than any other type of fishing, but I'm an opportunist. I'm not too proud to use the most productive techniques for that body of water. Sorry ... Well, I'm a little bit sorry, but not a lot sorry.

Robin, you have mastered the techniques of spin-fishing and fly-fishing. We nailed the brookies, and our big fish was ten inches. That's a pretty nice brook trout for the ponds. They are slick and fat and full of sass and vinegar. That was two down, and two to go. We had actually accomplished the most difficult part of the trip on the first day. The brook trout and golden trout are the most elusive of the four.

It was dark, we were tired and hungry, and I'm ready for pizza. Then it's time for bed. We have a big day tomorrow. It's pizza time at Antoine's Pizza Parlor. We have dinner, a lively game of pool, and then we head back to the lodge.

It's up early the next day, and then we're off to the West Walnut River. We're staying close to the Walnut, where I've caught many brown trout in the eighteen- to twenty-two-inch categories. We want the best possibility for a fish of any size today. We can upgrade to a trophy-sized grand slam at another date.

I like to target browns earlier in the day or at dusk because, as I said, they're nocturnal and are either going to bed in the morning or getting out of bed for an evening bite. An eight- to nine-inch brown trout may not sound like much of a fish, but on light tackle, it's a kick in the pants to catch them. This is especially true if there are lots of them. We hammered them. They are bronze bulldogs that stay down deep unless they're hooked in shallow water. In this scenario, they are as acrobatic as a sailfish. That's three out of four species; we had one more to go.

We jumped back into the truck and had a quick bite to eat. We're on to Blue Creek. It's a bit of a drive back in there, up dusty dirt roads. There's lots of sage and cactus. There is an oasis of trees snaking through the valley down below. It's a sure sign of water. It's Blue Creek.

Blue Creek is a small but sometimes deep stream that changes complexion often. At times, it looks like a classic gravel-bottomed brook. At other times, it winds and twists through meadows. Sometimes it is a submerged forest of downed trees. You can see the brown trout and rainbows that measure up to twelve inches or so, relishing the protection of deep holes and logs, lots of logs. They sun themselves, it seems, and scatter at the hint of our shadow. It was a bit difficult to work in there, but that's where the fish were, so that's where we decided to lose tackle. Back in the logs is where we completed the grand slam. Our big fish was a fourteen-inch holdover rainbow trout. A holdover is a fish that had been planted in the creek the previous season and has made it through the gauntlet of opening day anglers in what is usually a popular body of water. It has healed a bit from the scars that occurred from rubbing the bottom fins in their long-forgotten, concrete rearing tank. Holdovers also take on wild trout savvy. These fish, when caught on four-pound test or on a four or five-weight fly rod, will challenge any twenty-inch bruiser on heavier gear. I've caught brutish fish in lakes whose fight couldn't rival these fish on ultra-light gear. We also caught a few smaller wild rainbows that day.

Now we thought that we had completed the grand slam, and after a celebratory dinner and a good night's sleep, it was day three and time to go back over the hill. We picked up a couple of grand slam t-shirts, had breakfast, and headed for home. I wanted to make just one small stop over the pass that is still at the higher elevations. There is a beautiful year-round snow runoff stream called Jones Creek. The ice-cold water tumbles into deep holes. One of these pockets held a thirteen-inch cut-bow that I snatched on a four-weight fly rod. A cut-bow is a hybrid fish that occurs when a rainbow trout and a cutthroat trout mate. Cutthroat trout have two crimson slashes under either side of the throat. Hence we have the name cutthroat. This was the bonus fish and a final parting gift from God. Hopefully this was a weekend that you'll remember for years to come. I know that I will.

You might ask, "That's a great story, and it was a great adventure, but what does it have to do with living the Christian life?" That's a very good question.

I'll attempt to answer that question by using analogies from our story about trout fishing. For example, the different types of trout and the way that they crossbreed are very similar to what we currently see in Christian circles. There are many other pictures in this story that I hope to use to explain the pure strain of Christian thought. Before I do, I would like to tell you about an experience that I had some years back. This was the catalyst of a certain quest for truth.

First of all, I became a Christian over thirty-five years ago. Christ revealed Himself to me at a central California coast hamlet, and I gave my life and future to Him. I was truly born again. After twenty years of walking with Christ, and after having been miraculously changed, I'd also been beaten up pretty good, so to speak. I began to question what it was that I truly believed and what was biblical truth. After a couple of years of studying this in depth, I chose to process the information in seven letters to your sister, Lindsay. I touched on this earlier. After much study, I concluded that there were indeed but a few schools of thought and that they could be categorized for lay people like me. I also concluded that within Christianity, there really were some fundamentals that we could all agree upon, regardless of what flavor of denomination or movement we belonged to. I'll discuss these issues here shortly. These are the fundamentals of our faith. This series of events also marked the birth of your sister's letters and eventually of these letters.

We hear a lot of terms being thrown about like "cults," "world religions," "aberration or aberrant theology," and the list goes on. One Christian professor very simply draws the lines of delineation. He asks, "What do they do with the deity of Christ?" This is the foundation.

What is a cult? Webster says that it is a quasi-religious group with a leader who indoctrinates members with unorthodox or extremist views, practices, or beliefs. What is orthodox? It is conforming to the usual beliefs or established doctrines.

Let's simplify it even further. Fundamental truth is true truth. It's truth that all Christians can agree upon, regardless of sect or denomination. Let's define all else as "false teaching" and dispense with the rest. I feel that we don't necessarily have to name names and bust cults if we know the truth. If you have a working knowledge of Scripture and understand what the fundamentals are, when a counterfeit looms on the horizon, you'll identify it immediately. I think that this may be a different way of teaching on false doctrine. I'm not opposed to calling them out, but I think that many Christians are simply parroting what they are taught without embracing fundamental truths first and without doing their due diligence to learn God's Word on their own nickel.

Let's categorize these different schools of thought this way. A *false teaching* would be like a fake trout. An *aberration* is like a hybrid and *essential Christian doctrine* is like a pure strain salmonoid.

False teaching is like a fish that looks very much like a salmonoid, but is in reality an imposter. This doesn't make someone that is involved in a movement or a group that has false teachings a bad person. It just makes them responsible. They didn't do their due diligence to study the history of the movement or the founders (other than what their leaders told them). They didn't measure the beliefs against the yardstick of Scripture and they probably just believed what they were told by someone who they trusted. Sometimes it's as much as a few generations later that someone in the family begins to question these beliefs. Due to deep social, career, and emotional ties, it can be very difficult to break free from a group espousing false teachings. In this case, we really do become a product of whoever got a hold of us first, but it doesn't have to be that way.

When I was working in roofing supply distribution, I had a customer who was deeply involved in an international movement that was, of course, the only "true church." Let's call him Bill. He is one of the finest men I know and a businessperson with whom I have a great deal in common. I also have a lot of respect for him. We have similar political and business views, and he loves to hunt and fish. We are, however, diametrically opposed on the subject of biblical truth. He would often try to bridge the gap theologically, though he knew we differed. I avoided the subject for some time because I was processing the information to develop a polite but truthful response. Often, at our business breakfasts, his eyes would tear up, and he would try to open a conversation on the subject of religion. He didn't fully understand our differences. One morning, after I felt that I was prepared, he made his normal appeal to me for discussion before our business meeting. I gave him the audience that he desired. I closed my day timer and simply stated, "Bill, I believe that Jesus is God, and you don't." He did not argue the point, and that's the last discussion we've had on the subject to date. After he's chewed on that for a while, we'll pick it up again.

The sect, which he embraces, uses traditional Christian terminology but has a meaning other than that intended by the Christian church. The name of Jesus Christ and the term *savior* are commonly used with them, but they don't adhere to these terms from a biblical perspective. It's a semantics or language difference. They don't believe that Jesus is the one true God.

False teachers look like trout but are imposters.

An *aberration*, or deviation from essential doctrine, is like a hybrid.

They are a true salmonoid but have inbred with some questionable and false teaching. They may have *taken a nonessential and elevated it to the level of essential truth.* Using the term *hybrid* is a little weak of an analogy, but I think that you get the point. You can't breed a trout with a bass. The five dollar theological term for this is *syncretism.*

You can identify a hybrid Christian by his adherence to a specific soapbox or by some secret truth that is folded into his Christianity. These believers may indeed be Christians, but they are in danger of going off the deep end. They may just alienate themselves from the rest of their Christian brothers and sisters through self-righteousness, spiritual arrogance, or exclusivity. I've seen it go both ways.

A good biblical example of hybridization is Solomon. Solomon was King David's son, and he became king after David. He was clicking along just fine for a while as a godly believer. He was building on his dad's foundation. Solomon was considered the wealthiest and wisest man in history, but he didn't pay attention to one simple instruction: "Don't marry heathen women." Well, Solomon didn't just disobey the command. He did it up right. He married over one thousand wives or concubines. They led him completely away from the God of his fathers, and his final legacy was pretty dismal. The kingdom was carved up into pieces, and his final, closing words that were documented in the book of Ecclesiastes were quite depressing. His was a departure from the essentials, and it illustrates the importance of sticking to the basics. Can you now see how important that practical theology is to successful daily living?

What does a wild fish look like? What is essential, historic, conservative Christian doctrine? How was it determined to be just that? Pay very close attention.

These issues have been wrestled with since the beginnings of the birth of the church. Jesus Christ was clear about it. Heresy is departure from the truth. Nearly all of the epistles in the New Testament address and target the subject of foundational truth and of specific heresies.

As the church evolved, several councils met to determine truth. All Scripture defines, denies, or is obscure about it. That which is defined is truth. That which is denied is not, and that which is obscure yet does not contradict truth is negotiable. This is very important, so don't let this one slip by you. So is the simple list of essential Christian doctrine.

This is *essential Christian doctrine:*

+ The deity of Christ. Jesus Christ is and was fully God, though He became fully man. He was begotten and was not created.
+ The divine inspiration, infallibility, and inerrancy of Scripture. The Bible is and was divinely inspired by God. In its original form or autographs, it is without error and is infallible.
+ There is one God who expresses Himself in three distinct persons. There is one "what" and three "who's" in the Godhead. They are God the Father, God the Son, and God the Holy Spirit.
+ Jesus Christ was born of a virgin.
+ The sacrifice of the sinless Son of God was fully sufficient for our salvation from eternal damnation. We are saved by grace alone, through faith alone, in Christ alone.
+ We must individually accept Jesus Christ as our personal savior.
+ We believe in the fallen nature of all mankind and our need for a savior.
+ We believe in the church, a body of true believers in Christ that is not restricted to any particular denomination or movement.
+ We believe in the ordinances of the Lord's Supper and in believers' baptism.
+ We believe in the soon-coming return of Jesus Christ.
+ We believe in the resurrection of the dead. Those who have received the second birth will rise to eternal glory with Christ, and those who have rejected Christ will face eternal damnation.

Rob, there are a lot of ways that this has been stated in the form of creeds. It is listed on the backs of millions of church bulletins every Sunday that state, "What We Believe." I think that this pretty well sums it up, though. Now you get the lifelong opportunity to verify if this is indeed foundational truth or not. You also get to see how it is often cleverly twisted, as well as how many Christians major in minors and make our salvation into "Jesus plus some other items." It's vital to understand and to be able to identify false teaching. We must recognize if anyone adds to or subtracts from essential Christian doctrine. If your radar goes up because something other than the basics is being overemphasized or ignored, it's time to start asking questions. If someone or some group begins to emphasize an added book as inspired, or if the respect of a leader seems to be a bit more than it ought to be, don't be shamed into feeling foolish or overly skeptical. It's your life, and you only have one.

Regarding nonessentials, I'm not suggesting that other issues aren't important. The church, or body of Christ, expresses itself in a multitude of ways. I truly believe that these differences are mostly cultural though.

Well, that's what a wild trout looks like. Most important (and let my "catch and release only" brothers see this as an analogy), that's what a wild trout tastes like. What is the flavor of a vibrant, daily, practical walk with Christ?

As a little aside, I want to talk about planted fish. I was in a sort of Christian hot house for the first few years of my walk with the Lord. Just as a tomato that was raised in such regulated and controlled environment doesn't quite have the flavor, I didn't quite have the snap. I was a Christian, and yet my relevance was a bit weak. The marketplace or working world has been a good thing for me. It's toughened me up and tested me and forced me to grow up in some practical matters. The fins that were rubbed from the concrete holding tanks have pretty much healed, and I feel that I look and act more like a wild trout than a planter. I guess you would say that I'm a holdover.

By the way, this could also become dangerous if not carefully monitored. Our family has owned wild or feral cats. The domestication has been completely bred out of them. You can't tame them, and they are dangerous. They also carry diseases. Like Christians who can be infected by false teaching or bitterness or sin, they just don't play well with the other children. I've gotten close to being a feral Christian.

This was one of my favorite adventures. We've caught numerous grand slams since, but this was the first. I've caught grand slams where the fish dwarfed these in size, but this was the one where you were eight years old and we shared it together.

Speaking of pure-strain animals, I've been looking into a pure-strain European or Russian Boar trip. I guess it will never stop until I'm sitting in a wheelchair while you turn the pages of the journal.

JURASSIC PORK
RUSSIAN BOAR MISSION ACCOMPLISHED

Rob, I'm proud of you.
Love, Dad

BACK TO THE BASICS

> "All scripture is God breathed and is useful for teaching, rebuking, correcting and training in righteousness so that the man of God may be thoroughly equipped for every good work." (II Timothy 3:16 NIV)

Dear Robin:

Once a legendary coach had a dilemma. His team was in a real slump. At the half time of one particular game, he met with them in the locker room, held up the ball, and said, "This is a football." He wasn't being sarcastic. As in football, hunting, fishing, golfing, and all of life's endeavors, there are fundamentals. They have to be discovered, studied, applied, adhered to, and revisited often.

I was thirteen years old when I discovered trout fishing. I ran with a group of kids, some of whom ended up not being such great compadres. On one particular evening, we were staying up all night, and we got this harebrained idea: let's go fishing. We had one big problem: none of us knew how to fish. I found an old fiberglass fly rod with reel that my older brother had left behind when he joined the navy.

I lived in a small community in upstate New York. In the summer, you could go out at night with flashlights and find night crawlers everywhere, sort of basking in the moonlight on top of the grass, mating. If you would walk really slowly and move really fast, you could ruin their romantic interlude by snatching one and holding it as close to where it came out of the ground as possible. Then, if you pulled him out slowly and carefully, you'd have a nice big worm to use for fishing. By this time, Mrs. Worm would have quickly retreated back to her living room.

There used to be a hunting and fishing club on the outskirts of our town that apparently didn't survive. They planted pheasants, and they stocked a small brook with eastern brook trout. No one had fished in this little brook for many years, and the fish had reproduced naturally. I think that the state was also still stocking it. This is where the Rat Pack decided to try our luck at something that none of us knew anything about. There was Rick, Pat, Andrew, myself, and others I don't remember. Many years later, heroin got the best of Rick; he's no longer among us. Pat was my best friend. He emigrated from Italy and initially didn't speak a lick of English. Pat is a very loyal friend and a really nice guy. He finally went back to Italy, got married, and brought his bride back to the States. They still live here, and he has a couple of great kids. Andrew left home, started working for a Southern Californian city, and in time became the assistant city manager. He invested in a little hole-in-the-wall health food store over twenty-five years ago that now has several locations, and it has grown to over $100 million per year in sales. Andrew is wealthy now. And I joke with him that he still can't fish. We talk regularly. He's also a great guy and has become a believer.

We took our can of worms and fishing rods and headed on down the road, walking to Rambling Brook. Standing on the bridge, with fly rod in hand, I caught what was my first beautiful brook trout. I didn't know whether it was even a trout. I didn't know what a trout looked like and, besides that, it was a pretty poorly lit area. The only light was a streetlight that must have been one that we hadn't shot out with our BB guns. I knew that the fish was eight to ten inches long and had beautiful spots. The spots were a wonderful powder blue with pink in the middle. I believe that we released it and went on doing whatever it was that we were not supposed to be doing in the middle of the night.

That was my introduction into the world of trout fishing. This was well over fifty years ago. These friends mostly faded from the sport, but I became addicted to the species and to trout angling. Every day after school, I was fishing and studying the habits of these fish. It became a true obsession for me. I would read about them and draw them, and before long I think I began to grow scales and fins.

Childhood was pretty lonely for me for a number of reasons. My parents were divorced when I was very young, and I rarely saw them. So I was running the streets by the time of this trout event. I hope you feel really sorry for me by now because I'm about to ask to borrow money. The point is that trout fishing and art became my life. I'm the youngest of a family of seven children, but they had all pretty much moved out by this time. I had some friends, but they weren't trout fishing addicts like me.

I learned a few things about trout. They love colder water. They always face upstream, waiting to feed and assimilate the oxygen. They prefer clean, moving water. This is especially true of brookies. They primarily dine at daybreak and at sunset. They hide in the cover of undercuts in banks, and, if in the open, they prefer riffles and broken water for oxygenation and visual protection from birds of prey. They hang in feeding lanes. This is where feed floats by in its greatest concentration. There are a number of fundamentals, but one thing is for sure: If you can see them, they can see you. That is, of course, unless you are below them and they are facing upstream. Another fundamental is that they are smart. With the largest frontal lobe of any freshwater fish, trout are very intelligent.

Since those early years, I have gone on to catch thousands of trout and salmon all across the United States. By learning these fundamentals, I have caught hundreds of trophy fish and even several record-book fish. When I get in a slump, I remember to go back to the basics and, low and behold, my luck changes. What a coincidence.

MACKINAW TROUT

LAHONTON CUTHROAT TROUT

FUNDAMENTALS

I have witnessed a disturbing characteristic among those of the church in the West. Even though we have the greatest concentration of churches and Bibles and Christians anywhere, the majority of Christians have a very poor working knowledge of God's Word. They really don't understand the fundamentals. I'm not only talking about the theological fundamentals, as discussed in another letter. This is also true. I'm talking about a biblical worldview that comes as the result of a regular, daily, systematic ingestion of God's Word. Most Christians have never read the Bible from cover to cover.

They don't filter personal, family, or business decisions through the prism of God's Word. They primarily use the world's system to determine their future. Like the blind hog that occasionally stumbles onto an acorn, it is my opinion that they occasionally stumble onto the truth. They are, however, generally Christians with a secular worldview in many areas. They do not know what the books of the Bible are or where they may be found. They're living on the predigested spiritual food of the sermons that they heard last Sunday. Mommy bird is feeding baby bird a worm. The thing is, that baby bird is a full-grown adult in diapers. They are basically biblically illiterate. Now don't get me wrong; you know that I'm a man of the church. I believe strongly in church. I am also a firm believer in pastoral leadership. I support the concept of and attend the local assembly, but spiritual immaturity is epidemic.

We're going to chat a bit about what a football is, so to speak. We're going to study the history, structure, various translations, and ways to read through the Bible from cover to cover that have served your mom and me very well.

BIBLICAL WORLDVIEW

To catch a trout, you have to think like a trout. To think like a trout, you have to study trout. What is a biblical worldview? Let's assume that I have a portrait of da Vinci's *Mona Lisa* and you don't know that, because I have covered it with a piece of cardboard. The cardboard has a cutout of a circle large enough to expose only an eye. It would take an expert to know that this is anything more than just an eye, but when the cardboard is removed, you will see that it's the Mona Lisa. A biblical worldview is something like that. The Bible is a series of books that are linked together, like a puzzle or quilt, that convey certain basic principles that agree with themselves. If we have a good working knowledge of the whole picture, we can make any of life's decisions based upon God's view of things.

Jesus put it like this when He said, The kingdom of heaven is like yeast that a woman took and mixed into a large amount of flour until it worked all through the dough. A biblical worldview is very much like this. After having read through God's Word from cover to cover several times, it becomes a part of your very fiber. The Bible permeates your decision-making and thought processes. As you know, I have read the Bible through from cover to cover over forty times. I'm not saying this to brag, but to illustrate that I'm living what I'm preaching.

For example, when I wanted to marry, there was a certain set of guidelines that, if I followed them, would give me the best shot at marital success. Is she a believer? Does she have a history of putting God first in her life? Are her life's goals for career, ministry, and family the same as mine?

There are others, but these are some Bible-based fundamentals, and they permeate all of the books of the Bible and don't contradict them. If these principles are not adhered to, success is a bit of a gamble.

A biblical worldview is the way that the Jews have viewed life. The Bible is basically a Jewish book. It is broken into two parts. There is the Old Testament, which was primarily written in Hebrew, and the New Testament, which was written in common Greek. The earliest Christians were Jewish. The primary language that was spoken in Jesus's day was street Greek. In addition to this, small portions of the Old Testament were written in Aramaic. There are sixty-six books in all. The Old Testament was written before the time of Christ, and the New Testament was written after Christ walked the earth. There are thirty-nine books in the Old Testament and twenty-seven in the New Testament. *Testament* simply means "covenant or agreement."

Who wrote the Bible? Various men wrote it at different times in history. The Old Testament was written over a period of about one thousand years. It is a narrative of events that occurred over several thousand years. As stated, the Old Testament was primarily written in Hebrew but was translated into Greek at about the third century AD. This translation is called the Septuagint.

Moses wrote the first five books of the Bible. They are called the Pentateuch or the Torah. Tradition assigns the Books of History to Ezra or Nehemiah. King David wrote the majority of the Psalms. His son, Solomon, wrote most of the Proverbs and is believed to have written Ecclesiastes and the Song of Songs, or Song of Solomon. It is uncertain who wrote Job. The Major and Minor Prophets were written by their titleholders. Isaiah wrote the book of Isaiah, etc.

It is pretty well agreed upon who wrote the books of the New Testament. Their titleholders wrote the four Gospels. Luke also wrote Acts. Paul wrote the Pauline Epistles. They are Romans, I and II Corinthians, Galatians, Ephesians, Philippians, Colossians, I and II Thessalonians, I and II Timothy, Titus, and Philemon. It is uncertain as to who wrote Hebrews and Jude. Most believe that Paul wrote Hebrews, though some think it may have been Barnabus or Apollos. Jewish history attributes the writing of Jude to Jesus's biological brother, and James to another of Jesus's biological brothers. The Apostle John wrote I, II, and III John and the book of Revelation. The Apostle Peter wrote I and II Peter.

Did God write the Bible? The answer is yes, but He did not pen it as we might think. These authors were not in some hypnotic trance. The key is found in what the King James Version calls "inspiration" or what the New International Version calls "God breathed." In translation, this is not the same as our English word *inspiration*. It means that God so superintended the writing of Scripture that the authors wrote what He wanted them to write, yet were kept from error in doing so. God, the Holy Spirit, moved these men, yet they maintained their own personalities and writing styles. The Bible was actually expired by God, not inspired. It is incredibly consistent with itself and closely follows the rules of canonization. The Bible itself is inspired, not the men who wrote the Bible.

CANONIZATION

What is canonization? How was it determined what was and was not to be included as Scripture? *Canon* means "ruler" or "measuring rod." The Bible is its own Supreme Court. The concepts in the books must agree with themselves. It interprets itself. The rules for canonization were as follows: The books that are considered Scripture were required to be in harmony with those books about which there was no doubt. There was no doubt about the books of Moses in the Old Testament. There was no doubt about the book of Matthew. An apostle of Jesus Christ wrote it. Canon required that a book be harmonious with these benchmark books.

TRANSLATIONS

The original manuscripts are called *autographs*. They are considered inspired, not the translations. Though they no longer exist, God has maintained supernatural consistency in the oldest known manuscripts that do exist. Please note that there are changes in word meaning between the ancient languages and English. English words also undergo an evolution in meaning. Some of the words that mean one thing to my generation mean something else to yours. The most recent translations attempt to transcend these language barriers in the ancient languages of Greek, Hebrew, and Aramaic. For example, the difference in current word meanings is why the King James Version confuses some. Even though it is an English translation, it was written many centuries ago.

I believe that the New International Version is a good "thought for thought" translation, and the New American Standard is a good "word for word" translation. I generally read and study in the New International Version. I believe that the Amplified Bible is good for comparative study against other English translations. I memorize in the King James Version for poetic value, if the original meaning is there.

HOW DO WE STUDY THE BIBLE?

On the subject of "back to basics," I firmly believe that as serious Christians, we need to memorize the fact that there is an Old and New Testament with ten categories. Memorize them. I feel that a committed Christian should then memorize the titles of the sixty-six books of the Bible. I further feel that prior to or including any serious study, we should read the entire Bible from cover to cover. To read the Bible through in approximately five years, you would read one chapter per day. For ease of reading, I'd suggest that you begin with Matthew, and then read through to Revelation. Next, begin at Genesis and read through Malachi. If you do decide to embark on the one-year program, and after getting into it you feel it is too much for you at the time, I'd suggest a two-year or a five-year reading program. These can be obtained from the Internet or I will give you one.

In addition, it really helps to have a Bible reading partner. I am privileged to have your mom as mine. One of the great enemies of this discipline is discouragement. Accountability and encouragement really help you to be successful in reading through the entire Bible. You can read separately and compare notes.

My friend, Pastor Wayne Cordieiro, has written a great book on systematic Bible reading. By the way, his book *The Divine Mentor* is among my top ten favorite books. I'd strongly recommend that you read this.

Ask God to internalize what you have seen in Scripture by observation and ask Him to help you to apply it. In my decades of reading through the Bible from cover to cover, I have identified three major reasons why we as people don't finish this discipline after having begun.

#1: STUDY

Don't get bogged down in study. I know that this doesn't sound very spiritual or scholarly, but it is a common trap to get sidetracked for a day, a year, or a lifetime in deep study. Believe me, I know of what I speak. I've been doing this for a long time.

What I'm about to say is very important, so listen carefully. We currently attend a church where the Bible is taught in an expository manner. There are two types of teaching: expository and topical. Topical, or topic-based teaching is expressed by taking a subject and discussing it based upon Scriptures from various areas of the Bible and using other examples. It is good, if the teacher has solid views and is intellectually honest about his subject. This approach can most easily be abused if the teacher has a soapbox that isn't God's soapbox. He can major in the minors, but can also express incorrect views that prey upon the ignorance of new or immature believers. Expository teaching is exposing God's Word in context and in the order that it's given to us.

#2: GUILT

When we fall behind, we feel guilty, get discouraged, and quit. It is very normal to fall behind. Don't be too hard on yourself. It takes a while to create a habit. Experts say it takes twenty-five to thirty days. If you fall behind, you can make a note of what you missed and start where the schedule says you are to be reading today. Go back and clean it up on the weekend or when you're sitting by the pool while on vacation. Let's say you never go back and clean this up. Isn't it better to have read the majority of the text in a year's time than to quit?

#3: PUNCHING THE CLOCK

Please don't make an assumption about what I'm about to say. A common thought that we allow ourselves to indulge in is that if we are mechanically reading our assigned text daily and not getting anything out of it, we are wasting our time.

First of all, who are we to assume that if we are ingesting God's Word, which is alive and powerful and sharper than any sword through our eye gate, that it isn't accomplishing that which He pleases and prospering in the thing that He sends it to, piercing even to the dividing of our thoughts and intents and motives? The principle Scriptures are found in Hebrews 4:12 and Isaiah 55:11. By the power of the Holy Spirit, God's Word is doing its job and will be there in your subconscious memory banks when you need it.

You have seen me go through extreme trials in this life. Whether you saw them as extreme or not, they were about all that I could handle. We all go through them. It is promised to us. Jesus said in John 16:33: "In the world you will have tribulation, but be of good cheer. I have overcome the world" (KJV). None of us is immune or insulated from troubles of all kinds. "The rain falls on the just and the unjust" (KJV) It falls on Christians and non-believers. We are instructed by Paul in Ephesians 6:13–14 to "Stand in the evil day" (KJV). When the evil day of trials, temptations, and tribulations come upon us, our ability to understand them and navigate through them like a sailor in rough seas will be directly proportional to how much of God's Word we have hidden in our hearts. The Holy Spirit has to have something to work with to define and equip us in these times. In addition to effectiveness and accuracy in the battle, velocity of spiritual growth will be determined by our previous willingness to invest in this discipline. The trials are coming. Why not escalate the time it takes to endure and to overcome if we can?

In the beginning stages of most lengthy disciplines, you don't always feel like doing it. Anyone in school or college understands this. I don't always want to get up and go to work. We cannot allow ourselves the luxury of an emotion-based relationship with this discipline. If we as Christians would understand that we can hear Him more accurately on a daily basis while punching the clock, we would have a much higher success rate in revelations and the miraculous interventions of the Holy Spirit. Don't be a baby about this or you will stay an infant in Christ.

The rule of thumb is context. We understand Scripture in context with the chapter. We compare it to the book, and we see how our revelation stands up in context with all Scripture. Remember the Mona Lisa analogy.

It's been quite a journey. I really never thought that I'd last this long. In the words of World War I fighter pilots, "If I'd have known that I'd live this long, I'd have taken better care of myself." I am glad that I had a mentor with foresight. He loved me enough to guide me in this discipline, and it has served me very, very well.

Well, Rob, that does it. These are the Bible basics, and that's a football. Trout always face upstream. They love cold water, and there you have it. It's a great life.

Love, Dad

ADVENTURES IN PRAYER

> "Be careful for nothing; but in everything by prayer and supplication with thanksgiving let your requests be made known unto God. And the peace of God which passeth understanding, shall keep your hearts and minds through Christ Jesus." (Philippians 4:6–7 KJV)

Dear Robin:

I love Alaska. I pray that you will someday be able to go there. Just the thought of it brings to mind romantic pictures of adventure and wildness. As your mom and I draw closer to early retirement (hopefully), I pray that I'll be able to experience the adventure of the last frontier again. I'm hoping to kill a grizzly bear and that it will be in Alaska.

In the early eighties, an opportunity was presented for me to fish Alaska. Your sister was a toddler, and money was very tight. We lived in central California and worked full-time in recovery ministry. I had a good friend named Murry, who was an American-born son of a Sicilian. He was a squid fisherman, but the family held a license and kept a salmon boat moored in Alaska. Nearly one-third of all of the salmon in the Pacific congregated in this area of Alaska before returning to their natal rivers and streams to spawn and die. The short salmon season can be extremely profitable for commercial fishermen. It lasts, on average, about one month.

Murry presented a very attractive opportunity to me. He had a squid booth that he set up for various weekend festivals where he, with family and friends, would sell baskets of deep-fried calamari. Calamari is squid for the politically incorrect. He holds deeply guarded secret recipes for the delicacy.

It was a great hit at the festivals. Murry needed his booth painted with graphic art. He said that he'd pay for me to come to Alaska, to sport fish for trout and salmon, in trade for painting his booth. I signed up immediately.

I think giving you a little insight into the personality of Murry is important to the story. He was five feet, ten inches tall, and weighed two hundred and fifty pounds or more. Murry was a bodybuilder who could bench press twice my weight. He was a new convert to Christianity with a bit of a past. My first encounter with Murry was on the wharf. When I was introduced to him, he was selling fresh fish at his uncle's open-air fish market. He reached into the white bait bucket and plucked out a five-inch baitfish. He then bit its head off, chewed it up, swallowed it, and shook my hand. "Glad to meet you," he said. I liked Murry immediately. He was testing me. That's Murry. If you look in Webster's Dictionary for the definition of *enthusiasm, impulsiveness, energy, compassion* and *generosity*, it will say "Murry."

As a birthday present to me, Jackie helped me paint the booth. We airbrushed it in the most brilliant of colors, with a giant squid wrapped around the booth and other relevant graphics. It looked great. I have a photo of it somewhere.

ALASKA

The date arrived, and I left for Alaska with nothing more than about fifty dollars in my pocket and your mother, sister, and grandfather waving good-bye. It was July of 1984.

We landed in Anchorage, where there was a pretty good nip in the air and a lot of excitement. I was not a hunter at this time, but I clearly remember what may have been the largest, ten-foot Kodiak brown bear on the planet, standing in the airport, encased in glass. You won't find one of those in a California airport. After a layover of an hour or so, we boarded a smaller plane headed for Alaska, where I was to meet Jerry and catch a taxi to the cannery. Murry was going to meet me there.

Anticipation can often be disappointed by the actual experience. I was soon to find out that this wasn't going to be the case here. This airport was not an international airport or even a regional airport. It was smack dab in the middle of a lot of flat nothing. As I got off the small aircraft and unloaded my bag and fishing rods, I noticed that there was no Murry. It was nine o'clock at night, perfectly light out, and there was no Murry. Now this is the part of Murry's makeup that is not so charming. I waited and I waited and still, no Murry. I soon began to figure out that there was going to be no Murry.

Now, a taxi there is not like a taxi in a big city. It's an old van, driven by a college student who took the summer off to make some extra money by driving taxi. I hailed a taxi, and the driver, who was a female, inquired as to where I needed to go. You see, Alaska is a place where men are men and women are men, and they drive fast on rural dirt roads and they all carry side arms. I said that I needed to go to the cannery.

I arrived at what appeared to be a ghost town. There were a number of run-down wooden buildings. It was dusty and dirty, barren and windy, I discovered, all of the time. By now it was 10:00 p.m. and still light out. Now that will mess you up. You're tired, lost, alone, and on a foreign planet where there is no night. I did find a human though. It was the only one on planet Rural Alaska. He was an elderly Italian man who didn't speak one word of English. He was sitting in the mess hall, watching the children's channel. I found out later that he was watching the only channel that they got. Apparently, this channel was also a favorite among non-English-speaking fisherman. They watched it while playing poker and drinking whiskey. Somehow, I found out from him which building was ours, and I made my way over there to drop my gear off.

THE LUXURY HOTEL

Here it was, a magnificent edifice of architecture. It was a ramshackle, dilapidated, wooden building in desperate need of a paint job. I couldn't get in. The doors were all locked. The windows had no frames for me to get any leverage and they were very high. I did manage to get some sort of a foothold and got to a window to pry it open. I wiggled my way in, and there, in "the lobby," was a metal bed frame with springs. What lavish accommodations. I was cold, and I was exhausted. The doors to all of the suites were locked, so I laid down on the bedsprings to take a nap. It was windy out, and it was late, and the breeze and chill somehow permeated the building as well as my bones. With no pillow but my duffel bag and no blanket, I shivered. I just couldn't sleep.

Fact is sometimes stranger than fiction, and this is not an embellishment of fact. I'd like to say that this was a wonderful adventure, but you know me better than that. I was not having fun, but I was in Alaska. I knew that something good could happen because it was there for the happening. I just hadn't cracked the code yet. Murry made it a bit more interesting. I guess they didn't have paper and pencil in Alaska to leave notes of explanation.

Because I couldn't sleep, I went for a walk on this new planet called Rural Alaska. What's that about anyway? I was soon to meet another resident alien on my little stroll on the beach.

THE BEACH

This wasn't the Caribbean, to be sure. The tide was out. The temperature was in the mid to high thirties. I then saw ATVs all over the beach with little carts in tow. They were stopping at various points and picking up salmon off the beach. This five-foot-tall native Alaskan girl barked orders at the men. To say that it was surreal would be an understatement. I figured that she was the boss, so I went over to her and began to ask questions. Time is money in Alaska and time is short during the salmon run, so she made it quick. The salmon came in early. The magistrates blew the whistle for the games to begin, and everyone was there laying out their nets. She was a gill fisherman. Murry and the rest of the armada were laying out sets of lumpata. Lumpata is also a type of gill fishing, but the nets are set in deeper water by boat. What I was witnessing was a type of commercial fishing where you lay out gill nets by hand from shore at low tide. You then allow the tide to rise, and traveling fish get caught in the nets. When the water recedes again, you gather the catch from the beach. The interview was over.

MURRY

Good old Murry. I went back to the lobby and had managed to get a little sleep when the door crashed open and Murry arrived, out of breath. He showed me to my room and pointed to the bed and to the fishing rods in the corner. He said the fish were in and he had to go, shoved a wad of a few hundred dollars cash into my hand, and told me that I should call a taxi tomorrow.

"Tell them to take you to the King Salmon River in the morning and set a time to pick you up in the evening. You'll catch reds and rainbows. Use this salmon roe. Then take a taxi the next day to the Nu Nuk River. Rent a boat and ask someone how to fish it. I've got to go. I'll be back before it is time for you to fly home." Well, at least I was going fishing.

The next day I called a taxi and did as Murry said. The female taxi driver dropped me off at the bridge, and I trudged through the muck below to a small feeder stream. I plopped my little bait into that stream, and immediately it was attacked with a vengeance by what seemed like a school of piranhas. It was a group of over one hundred wild rainbow trout that topped out in size at about twelve inches. These weren't the monster-sized leopard trout that I'd read about that go over fifteen pounds, but it sure was fun. I did that for a while and headed over through the swamp to the King Salmon River.

King Salmon River is a moderately sized river: fifty to one hundred yards wide, with lots of dense brush up and down both sides. I had an ominous feeling because I was alone. The water was very low, so I cast a big spoon that I'd found by the river, to likely holes and riffles. Not much happened for a while, and then, while casting to a broad, flat area, the spoon just stopped. It suddenly rose straight up three feet into the air with a ten-pound sockeye salmon attached. It was pretty fresh for a sockeye in the river. It doesn't take awful long for them to color up after they enter the fresh water. They are, in my opinion, the most colorful of spawning salmon. I've caught and seen them with candy-apple-red bodies and bright olive-green heads. A male can have a hooked jaw with doglike teeth so predominant that you begin to wonder if it isn't capable of stalking you like a dangerous game animal. But these sockeyes were still pretty bright, which made them a better bet for good table fare. Sockeyes are actually considered the best eating salmon and command the best prices at market. The commercial fishermen call them "reds" due to their bright red-orange meat.

I moved on down the creek and soon saw a fellow on the opposite side who was also fishing. He had a very large pistol on his hip. He looked like a movie star and, given the fact that I was in an alternate universe, he may have been one. He said that he worked for Constance Engines and that the .44 Magnum was for bears. They were also there with us. I made an executive decision and asked permission to fish with him. Thankfully he said yes. He showed me the ropes, and I soon caught a king salmon over twenty pounds. What a thrill this was in a shallow river like that one. Before long, he had to go back to something or other, and I was on my own again with the bears. I devised a plan. If a bear were to pursue me, I'd throw my salmon and keep moving. It sounded logical to me. Knowing what I do now about bears, a .44 Magnum is a far better plan. It sure did seem like a long trip back to the bridge, the taxi, and the Amazon of a driver. She picked me up on time, and we headed back to hotel.

I don't remember where I ate, but I must have. It was probably room service at the hotel or maybe at one of the restaurants with fine cuisine on the property. After a good night's sleep, I hooked up with my taxi the next day to rent a boat at the Nu Nuk River.

NU NUK RIVER

I was brought to a marina that was just a few miles from where the river left the huge expanse of Alaska. I was not that far from Russia at this time, which was then called the USSR, and that seemed pretty cool. The fishing technique that I used was to get in line with the other boats as the river floated through the run, down to the end of and out of the hole. I bounced roe off the bottom, and they said I'd know if I got a hit. I got pretty comfortable with the whole thing, and everything went fine until something that I didn't anticipate happened. I hooked a fish. These are fresh, powerful fish, and there is a reason they call them king salmon. They're big. They are the largest of all salmon species. They can grow to in excess of one hundred pounds, and they fight like bulls. I fought this fish with one hand and tried to steer the small aluminum boat with the other. I hadn't yet figured out the last part. How was I going to land it? It wasn't long before my arm grew tired and my boat wasn't exactly doing what I wanted it to. I got this slab of a silver fish up to the side of the boat and somehow got a gaff into its head and dragged it over the gunwale of the tiny boat. The fun continued as he thrashed about with brute strength and bled an awful lot. He weighed thirty-three pounds. That's a good fish by Nu Nuk standards, but a huge fish by mine. I did this for quite a while. I then took a break and went back to the marina.

THE LAWYER

That's where I met the lawyer. This fellow had been hired by some Japanese fishermen to negotiate buying salmon from the American fishermen. He had come by commercial plane with one million dollars of their cash in a back pack to buy salmon. I'm quite sure that they wouldn't allow this today. The Japanese were not allowed to come ashore, so this transaction all took place on a Japanese processing boat in the bay. After his work was finished, he took a day or so to do a little salmon fishing. We decided that it might be better if we went out on the next go-round together. It was now after midnight, and it was still light out. I love Alaska in July. It wasn't too bad until I began to out-fish him. He was a very competitive sort. By the end of this little adventure, his determination was to catch a larger fish than I had, and he didn't. It was no longer fun, so I wrapped it up and went ashore. He did, however, make it clear when I saw him on the plane home that he had caught a fish larger than mine.

NU NUK DANGER

I had a brainstorm. I had my limit of salmon, so why not take the boat and go alone, up the Nu Nuk River to Nu Nuk Lake, to fish for dolly varden and rainbows. Bad idea. It was quite pleasant at first. Going down the river as it meandered through the tundra, I saw many bald eagles. I pulled over for a pit stop and walked on a thick carpet of tundra. Tundra is a moss that grows on ground that never thaws. I picked up a few souvenirs of flora and loaded myself back into the boat. I continued to travel farther. It's an odd thing to go mile after mile, around bend after bend, and see very little sign of human life other than a few boats. There were no houses, riverfront condos, or roads. An occasional floatplane hummed and buzzed overhead. I noticed something else that was curious. The other boats I saw were all small boats headed the other way, and the river was getting bigger and deeper and faster. The tide was rising. I never have much liked looking over the side of anything and being unable to see the bottom. I became especially concerned when I saw rapids ahead. It became windy, and the river got faster. Fishing became less important, and surviving became more important. I figured it was time to go back, and I did.

It was a long way back because it was windy and wavy and all upstream. I've been in similar situations in small craft on the ocean and also recently in Idaho. I really don't like it. It teaches you to pray in desperation. Well, after a few hours, which seemed like an eternity, I made it back to the boat ramp. I took a taxi to the hotel, and not long after that, Murry came back.

I had my one hundred pound maximum allowance of fish that was the airline's weight limit. Nu Nuk was a frightening experience, but is now a fond and nostalgic memory.

There were many other aspects to this adventure, but these are the highlights. There was the thirty-five dollar hamburger dinner (the last of my money) and a number of other events, but that's the gist of it.

This is very much like the adventure of prayer. It seems so trite to me when people view a relationship with God in prayer as a ritualized discipline where you punch in and punch out. I really don't have the time for that. If God is real and answers prayer, I want to see answers, and you know full well that I do. Sometimes He says yes. Sometimes He performs the miraculous. Sometimes He says no. Sometimes He says, "Wait," and sometimes He says nothing and He doesn't explain why He says nothing. You didn't expect that one, did you?

King David is one of the best role models of the adventure of a life lived in prayer with God. He was considered a man after God's own heart, and yet his days were filled with all of the elements of this trip. There was fear, frustration, and danger. There were mistakes, desperation, and miracles. This trip was a great example of God's provision, supernatural victories, and conquests to meet the demands of a young man (me) with a very high need for adventure. I've been experiencing it for decades and have come to expect His favor. This is God's nature, and I am so grateful for it.

We see the private self of David as he pours his heart out in the book of Psalms. We also see miraculous intervention and the personal attention that he had from a God with whom he had a close, personal friendship.

QUESTIONS

At this point, I'm going to deviate from a normal format and approach my points with questions, which I think might mix it up a bit. It seems like a good place to address a few items.

Question: What is prayer and how do we pray effectively?

Answer: Prayer is communicating with God as you would communicate with a friend. Private prayer needn't be pretty. It needs to be real. Sincerity is the first order of business. Hebrews 10:19–20 tells us that we can boldly enter the throne room of grace because of the sacrifice of Jesus Christ (KJV).

Question: How do we pray?

Answer: We pray effectively by talking to the Father, in the name or authority of the Son, through the Holy Spirit. Jesus gave the disciples a model prayer in Matthew 6:9–13. He said, "This then is how you should pray: Our Father in heaven, hallowed be thy name. Thy kingdom come. Thy will be done on earth as it is in heaven. Give us this day our daily bread. Forgive us our debts, as we also have forgiven our debtors. And lead us not into temptation, but deliver us from the evil one" (KJV).

ACTS

There is an awful lot there. I like the way Bill Hybels, pastor of the largest church in the United States, breaks the elements of this prayer into the simple ACTS acrostic. Pastor Hybels has given me permission to include this information.

"A" IS FOR ADORATION AND WORSHIP

Though He is our friend, He is God. We worship or honor His majesty in our heart but also out loud. Worship music is a great vehicle to carry the emotion that the Holy Spirit can bring to our hearts.

"C" IS FOR CONFESSION

There are two types of confession. We confess our sins, and we affirm His words. Recognizing our sinfulness and confessing it to God, and even to others when it's appropriate, maintains humility.

The Bible tells of a time when King David really messed up. God had elevated him from an unknown shepherd boy to the most powerful king on earth. One day, while cruising on his rooftop suite when he should have been out conquering, he saw this woman bathing below him on her roof. He had her brought up to his penthouse, got her pregnant, and killed her husband to cover up his sin. God punished him severely for this. The consequences were public. His reaffirmation was also done publicly after his private repentance that is found in Psalm 51.

We also confess by confessing and affirming His Word. We should determine as best we can whether a particular something is God's current will for us before we claim it. Thank God that He doesn't us everything that we want when we want it. There are, however, plenty of times He gives us more than we ask for.

Confession of this kind can be appropriate under certain circumstances, but a confession of His character traits goes a long way to helping us feel victorious. It puts us in the right frame of mind to receive from him.

"T" IS FOR THANKSGIVING

It may sound insignificant, but gratefulness is a tremendous vehicle to help us feel good about things apparently gone badly. I for one would include it in the arsenal of spiritual weaponry as a part of praying always, with all manner of prayer and supplication spoken of in Ephesians, Chapter 6. We are told to, "Count Your Blessings and Name Them One By One." The first chapter of Romans tells us that reprobation, or being without conscience, is largely the result of being ungrateful. Being thankful is very powerful. List your blessings out loud.

"S" IS FOR SUPPLICATION

Supplication is simply asking. We ask for others, and we ask for ourselves.

Asking for others is called intercessory prayer. It is a great discipline and can also be a passionate calling for some. It seems that the prayer warrior is often the little old lady who goes largely unnoticed. I could tell you stories that you might not even believe of intercessors who have moved men and mountains. They submit to God through prayer and fasting, and act as a support for many people who are on the front lines of ministry, so to speak. I have had a number of people in my life of this sort.

We ask for ourselves. James 4:2 says, "We have not because we ask not" (KJV). As I said, sometimes He says no, but how many have missed an experience simply because we haven't asked? I wanted to go to Alaska. Don't think that I hadn't asked.

Question: What are some hindrances to prayer?

Answer: Discovery is part of the adventure. There aren't any silver bullets or magic formulas or chants to guarantee total success in prayer, yet God gives us some clear guidelines to follow.

First of all, we pray, touching an invisible, spiritual world. It isn't some sort of metaphysical adventure into the Twilight Zone. It isn't weird, and we aren't weirdoes. I guess some people think that we are, but to me, they are the oddballs.

One clear hindrance to answered prayer is sin. David said in Psalm 66:18, "If I regard iniquity in my heart, the Lord will not hear me" (KJV). We need to keep short accounts with God.

We also need to keep short accounts with others. For example, I Peter 3:7 tells us that our prayers will be hindered if we are not in a right relationship with our spouse. Jesus also told us that if we think we're doing a great spiritual service to Him by giving or by praying, and know that we are not in a right relationship with our brother, that we need to first go get that right before we offer any gifts to Him. This is found in Matthew 5:24.

When we are getting it right with God, we know that our forgiveness is at hand because He says that it is. I John 1:9 says, "If we confess our sins, He is faithful and just to forgive us of our sins and to cleanse us from all unrighteousness" (KJV). We are forgiven because He says we are forgiven, not necessarily because we feel it. This is a great misconception in the Christian life. Feelings are unreliable.

Another hindrance to prayer is Satan. Satan and his angels can hinder our prayers. Daniel's prayers were being hindered by a very powerful demon. In Daniel, Chapter 10, during a season when Daniel was praying and fasting, God sent an angel to intervene, but it took three weeks for him to achieve victory over this enemy. God doesn't always respond to our schedule. He responds to His.

Fasting is a great tool to break the bonds of the enemy. Jesus instructed us on fasting in Matthew 6:16–18. It's also found in Mathew 9:14–19. Fasting voluntarily brings us to a condition of our greatest physical weakness. Fasting is self-imposed mourning. When Jesus was fasting in the great temptation in the wilderness for forty days and nights, it says, "He was hungry." Medically speaking, He was starving. This weakness, catalyzed by fasting, reveals any personal character obstructions. We pave a clear path or band wave of communication between God and ourselves by recognizing the sin and asking Him to forgive us of it and remove it. This is called "repentance." We have a huge tendency toward self-deception that is clarified with prayer and fasting. Many matters that were left undone are resolved. God also honors the very act of personal sacrifice in abstaining from food.

Question: What is the role of the Holy Spirit in prayer?

Answer: I knew that you would ask that question. I embrace the exercise of praying in tongues. Many who read this, possibly including you, may not embrace this teaching. However, if you study Scripture and church history, it is an orthodox or acceptable teaching. I elaborate on this in the letter on gifts.

First of all, for those of us who believe in this tradition, there is a function of the Holy Spirit that I'd call *devotional tongues*. We pray in tongues as a form of intercession and edification. Edification is being drawn closer to God.

Prayer is the Holy Spirit's territory, if you will. He guides us, convinces us of sin, and leads us. This is done by the confirmation of God's Word. Jesus said in John 16:13, "When the Holy Spirit would be given to us that he would guide us into truth" (KJV). He further stated in John 17:17, "Thy Word is truth." Pray the word. Confirm revelation by the mouth of two or more witnesses, one of which needs to be the Bible.

Question: What do we pray about?

Answer: I pray about everything. David said in Psalms 41:1–2, "As the deer pants for streams of water, my soul pants for you, O God. My soul thirsts for God, for the living God" (KJV). He's not too busy, and the worst that He can say is no. I don't feel guilty about praying about everything. I'll let someone else feel guilty.

Well, that's it for now. There is much to be said about prayer but I think these are the basics. We always run the risk of experiencing prayer in a sort of academic or hypothetical way. I love Jesus, and I know Him. The relationship is, in and of itself, prayer. Paul says in I Thessalonians 5:17, to pray without ceasing (KJV).

Robin, I hope that you are primed for adventure. A life of prayer is much like this excursion in Alaska. I love to pray, simply because I know that God answers prayer. Prayer is a great adventure.

Keep your hooks sharp and your powder dry.

Love, Dad

THE MOST DANGEROUS GAME

"The weapons that we fight with are not the weapons of the world. On the contrary, they have divine power to demolish strongholds." (II Corinthians 10:4 NIV)

Dear Robin:

In the summer of 2002, I got this wild idea that losing enough weight so I could hunt bear was next on the list. It's a very vigorous sport, and you have to be in good shape for it. Now, you know that when I get the idea that I want something, sooner or later, I prayerfully figure out a way to get it. That is, except for the times God does not have the foresight that I do to allow me to have a particular something.

My best guess is that we had been hunting for less than a year. As a matter of fact, it was more like six months. I've been angling now for over forty years. In your younger years, you had caught about every type of trout that could be caught and in about every situation. You were a little bored with it, and then you discovered guns. They were loud, dangerous, and you could kill stuff with them. I guess I can blame the origins of my passion for shooting sports on you.

Wouldn't you think that it is a natural progression to jump from cottontails, doves, pheasants, and quail to giant black bears?

I approached a fellow in the church that I knew hunted bears and asked if he would take us out. He said sure, and I went on a crash weight-loss program. The plan was to lose forty-five pounds in six months, to the tune of one to two pounds per week, and I'd be ready for November.

JOHN

Now, John Peacock is a dangerous guy. I soon found out that almost all bear hunters are pretty dangerous guys. A lot of them are quiet men, but they all are truly dangerous. They aren't macho men, just nice guys who are dangerous.

They travel in packs with an alpha male. They have military-like loyalty, and they're trained killers. The bear-hunting culture is unique. It takes on a whole new flavor when the leader is a Christian man who also happens to be dangerous to the kingdom of darkness. John is such a man. During John's tenure as a pastor at a large local church, over four hundred souls were snatched from the clutches of darkness to become Christians. John's demeanor quickly dispels the idea that Jesus is like a mild man in the neighborhood with a beard.

Well, sometime in November, I had fulfilled my goal of losing forty-five pounds, was at fighting weight, and we started the dry runs. These dry runs don't involve classrooms with paper and pen. They involved real bears, big bears.

There are essentially three types of bears in North America. They are polar bears, brown bears, and black bears. Polar bears live in polar regions and are primarily carnivores, growing up to fifteen hundred pounds. Brown bears are omnivores, and they can grow up to ten feet from tip to tail. The ten-footers are found in Alaska. These coastal bears can weigh over a thousand pounds. A grizzly bear is a type of brown bear, and they are also huge.. They no longer live in California due to human encroachment. North American black bears are also omnivores and will grow upwards of seven hundred pounds. Now, when I say that these bears grow up to these sizes, that's in world-classed sizes, not average sizes. Regionally, their size varies dependent upon genetics and length of growth seasons, but most hunters will never see a trophy approaching these sizes. A trophy black bear in Idaho is two hundred and fifty pounds or more, and in British Columbia it's over four hundred pounds. In 2002, we encountered a few in central California that went over four hundred. A bear of about four hundred pounds was our dry run. Black bears are especially dangerous if on the ground, wounded, or with cubs. This one was on the ground.

We hunt them with dogs that are trained to detect the scent of bears and tree them. This one didn't want to be treed. The monster boar (male bear) was cornered and battling it out with about five dogs. He was tossing dogs, as my friend Ned calls it, and had to be killed. One of the dogs was wounded and bleeding. Another dog had been killed a week or so earlier in a similar situation. They wouldn't let me go in on this one. Edward, a member of the team, went in on hands and knees under tall scrub oaks. They had .444 lever-action guide guns. I sat on a hill with Doug and John's brother. We had a bird's-eye view of the whole show. I didn't see the bear until after it was killed—only the evidence of a bear. I witnessed a trail of ten-foot oaks being shaken by what seemed like a veloceraptor scene and could not believe the speed with which an animal of that bulk could travel.

Well, it wasn't too long after this that there were a couple of cannon blasts that echoed through the hills. We received the report by radio that it was over, and the brute was dragged out by a winch.

After that experience, I wanted more. We did a few more weekends, and on the last weekend in November, we treed my bear. There were nine of us, including you. You were twelve years old, and you had also developed a bit of a taste for it all. Now, just because I was at fighting weight didn't mean that I was in fighting condition. This time we were in much more extreme terrain. It was a series of steep rock canyons. While traveling up and down logging roads by truck, the dog struck a scent. The strike dog stands in the back of the pickup truck on top of the dog boxes, and his job is to detect the smell of a bear. If it appears to be the real deal and not a false strike, all of the dogs are let out of the stainless steel dog boxes, and the race is on. Usually, the other trucks in the party have triangulated and are instructed to have at it and release their dogs also. That is, unless they are on another bear. The dogs have radio-controlled collars, and the driver has an antenna receiver that beeps loudest when pointed in the direction of the dogs. The signal strength determines the proximity of the dogs. If they stop for any length of time, the bear is probably caught.

Well, this bear was a couple of miles in there, or up there and down there. I would not have made it to the tree except for the encouragement of you and Jim, Doug's assistant. You said, "You can do it, Dad. You didn't put yourself through all of this to give up at the very end." We finally made it to the tree, or at least you guys did, and the bear bolted over the paved road and up another tree. We (rather I) dragged myself back up to the paved road and a few yards down a small dirt road. There was Doug, sitting on the dog boxes in the back of his truck, drinking a soda. He said, "Robin, your bear's in the tree. Go kill it." The bruin was less than one hundred yards from the main road—I'd guess thirty or forty feet up the tree, poised like a gorilla.

Within a short period of time, the whole team of nine was at the tree, and then I witnessed one of the weirdest cultural events that I can remember. The dogs kept the bear treed, and we all put our guns down for a photo opportunity. We took a variety of lovely pictures, while the beast watched. Then it was time. The dogs were roped at a distance, and with all guns on target, I was instructed to shoot. I was shooting a .30 caliber and about a 160-grain bullet. This is a placement gun versus a power punch gun. You intuitively didn't want to stand next to John and myself. You chose to place yourself a bit up the hill. I squeezed the trigger and put a bullet right behind his ear. He came tumbling down. It was a good shot, and the beast lumbered off to expire, with Edward's McNab shepherd dog, Bonzo, right in front of him. John drew his .44 Magnum revolver, stepped in front of me, and opened fire. Like a disturbed hive of angry African killer bees, the bear turned and charged right at us. John stood his ground and unloaded the pistol at close range into a standing, charging bear. John looked like a professional basketball player, leaning back and executing a jump shot while unloading the massive pistol in the enormous animal's face. *Boom, boom, boom, boom, click,* and the bear didn't go down, and then *kaboom!* Mike put the killing shot in his massive body from across the small ravine. The .444 with a 300-grain bullet did the trick.

There he lay, a massive pile of fat and fur. His canine teeth protruded an inch and a half from his gums and, when extracted, were three and a half inches long. His huge paws contained razor-sharp claws. One bat from his arm and he could easily have broken a man's neck. We had no idea just how big he was until he was weighed on a registered scale at the butcher. The monstrous beast weighed five hundred and sixty pounds, a gold medal bear, and was scored to rank number 21 internationally. He's standing in our living room, in the crook of the piano.

That was the day I decided to get a bigger gun. The .30 caliber was plenty of gun, but that was plenty of bear. Unlike some other big game, bears can take an awful lot of lead. I killed a trophy mountain lion this year in Nevada with a .223. I dispatched it with one shot; a heart lung shot at thirty yards. They don't take much lead. This bear had over three inches of fat and took as many as eight bullets.

There are three types of firearms. There are rifles, shotguns, and handguns. We hunt upland game, doves, and bunnies with shotguns. We use rifles and handguns for everything else. The idea with dangerous game is to use enough gun.

I like to hunt dangerous game because it's stuff that bites back. I like to hunt with dogs because it can be up close and personal. I feel that otherwise it may not be as dangerous, although sometimes it is. It can be technical, long-range shooting, which is also a lot of fun; but up close, you can feel their attitude, and bears, mountain lions, and wild pigs have attitude. There are two firearm philosophies in big game hunting. One is velocity for long distance and placement shooting. The other is knock-down power for close-range shooting. I now shoot a 45-70 for bears and hogs. It's a cannon. It's designed for grizzly bears and buffalo. It's what you used on your bear, Rob.

Well, that's the story. I didn't embellish it. If I weren't there, I probably wouldn't have believed that it happened. By the way, your choice to move up the hill a bit was a good one.

Spiritual warfare, as depicted in God's Word and as it plays out in real life, is also a very dangerous game. The text verse is worth repeating. As already stated in II Corinthians 10:4, "The weapons we fight with are not the weapons of this world. On the contrary, they have divine power to demolish strongholds" (NIV).

Who are we fighting as Christians and what are the weapons? First of all, we are fighting an enemy named Satan. Satan is not a concept or an allegory. He is a fallen angel that took one-third of the other angels with him when he fell from grace. This is found in Isaiah 14:17, and Jesus talked about it in Luke 10:18 and in Revelation 12:4. Satan attempted to overthrow the God of heaven, according to Scripture, and his targets are you and me.

Just as the dangerous game animals that we hunt are at home in their habitat, so too is Satan very much at home in this world. He should not be underestimated. He has had thousands of years to adapt. To compound the problem, He is also a spiritual being, not a physical one, so he is not visible to our natural eyes. One of His greatest deceptions is convincing us that he either doesn't exist, or minimizing himself by reclassifying him as a concept.

He has many names. They depict his character as well. He is "The accuser of the brethren," "The serpent," "The prince of demons," "The god of this world," "A roaring lion," "A thief that comes to rob, steal, kill, and destroy," "Destruction," "The father of lies," and the list goes on.

His minions are fallen angels called demons. They are his soldiers. They strategize under his direction to target your greatest potential weaknesses and to take you down or disable you.

This isn't a Hollywood film. This is a real battle with real consequences that are eternal in nature. As you can see, his objective is to destroy God's children. In my years of dealing with him, I have seen that his tactics seem to include disabling Christians rather than completely eliminating them. Let me explain.

The M-16 was the military weapon of choice. It's been said that the idea was that if there were a nonlethal shot, the bullet was designed to spin upon impact and tumble down the limb or torso to create a mess. This would, in effect, disable several soldiers who would have to attend to the wounded versus only one dead soldier. Does this sound anything like the local churches in the West?

The strategy of taking out Christians with scandal is also designed to dishonor the name of Christ. This is especially true of Christian leadership. I don't need to list the names of the wounded captains of Christendom that may never be effective for the Kingdom of God again.

Another strategy he employs is to cause Christians to become lukewarm in their walk with Christ. Our objective is to finish strong. He will patiently peck away at our fervor and discourage or secularize us, turning us into worldly, carnal Christians.

What are these weapons? The Scripture says in Ephesians 8–10:

> Finally, be strong in the Lord and in his mighty power. Put
> on the full armor of God so that you can take your stand
> against the devil's schemes. For our struggle is not against
> flesh and blood, but against the rulers, against authorities,
> against powers of this dark world and against spiritual forces
> of evil in heavenly realms. Therefore put on the full armor
> of God so that when the evil day comes, you may be able
> to stand your ground, and after you have done everything
> to stand. Stand firm then, with the belt of truth buckled

around your waist, with the breastplate of righteousness in place and your feet fitted with the readiness that comes from the gospel of peace. In addition to all this, take up the shield of faith with which you extinguish all of the flaming arrows of the wicked one. Take the helmet of salvation and the sword of the Spirit, which is the Word of God. And pray in the spirit on all occasions with all kinds of prayers and requests. With this in mind, be alert and always keep on praying for all saints. (NIV)

THE BELT OF TRUTH

Standing toe-to-toe with an angry black bear is no time to question the ethics of hunting. Hopefully you have already worked all of this out beforehand. When you are in a crisis, whether it's real or imagined, it's no time to question the existence of Satan. It is not the best time to become introverted and wonder what you have done to bring this upon yourself, especially if there are others involved. It's not time to negotiate. You don't negotiate with terrorists in this world or in the spiritual realm. As a man, it's time to man up and get after it.

What is the truth? First of all, Jesus said in John 14:6 that "He is the way, the truth and the life" (NIV). He is himself the truth. He also said in John 17:17 that "The Word is the truth" (NIV). This can be a bit tricky because Scripture can be taken out of the context in which it was meant to be understood. This is exactly what the enemy tried to do with Jesus when tempting him in the wilderness. The devil used Scripture out of context. Scripture must be understood within the context of that passage, that book, and the entire Bible. Others cleverly parse words by separating Jesus from His divine nature and by quoting those passages that call Him the Son of God, but not God incarnate. They ignore those Scriptures that assign deity. Jesus is God, and they might be using semantics to relegate Him to less than His position as the one true God.

One man encourages us to imagine a Roman soldier who has all of his clothing tucked into his belt. His entire weaponry hangs on his belt. We have everything riding on our grasp of the truth.

Your pistol and ammunition hang on the belt. Your knife hangs on the belt. At the critical juncture of true spiritual action, you must embrace as much of the truth as you know. You can refine your deep theological understanding and, like the bear hunting, you can ponder the minutiae of the sport later. Right now, it's important that the enemy does not see your backside—that is, unless you enjoy the tearing of flesh, the sight of blood, and the sound of crushing bones. I'm talking about your flesh, your blood, and your bones. I have seen the casualties and have come close to being one.

THE BREASTPLATE OF RIGHTEOUSNESS

Righteousness is a bit of a curious thing. The prophet Isaiah tells us in Chapter 64, Verse 6, that "We are all as an unclean thing and that all of our righteousness is as filthy rags" (KJV). On the other hand, Jesus says in Matthew 5:20 that unless our righteousness exceeds that of the recognized religious leaders, we won't see heaven. What's up with that?

First of all, what is righteousness? Webster defines *righteousness* as "acting in a justly upright manner." Upon receiving Jesus Christ as my personal savior and becoming born again, it has been my experience that I have acted in a perfectly upright manner from that very day forward and ever since. I'm speaking sarcastically. You know that this isn't so.

Historically, there are two brands of biblical righteousness. There is positional righteousness and practical deeds of righteousness. Let me explain.

Paul, the author of this text on the items of armor, probably took this piece of armament from Isaiah 59:17, which says, "He put on righteousness as a breastplate" (NIV). The prophecy is about Jesus Christ.

What is positional righteousness? Upon accepting Christ as savior by faith, a mystical thing happens in the spiritual realm. We have assumed His righteousness because ours is as filthy rags. That's why we need a savior from our sins. It's because of our unrighteousness. As with all of the items of armor, we should put them on in our mind when in emotional, spiritual, or circumstantial crisis, and even speak them out loud at times. Positional righteousness says that I'm righteous because I have Him inside of me and He is righteousness. This is much like the depiction of being raised with Christ in baptism. We accept this by faith, not by feelings. If you try to accomplish enough deeds to be righteous, the best that you will become is self-righteous.

Deeds of righteousness are just that. As Christians, we do deeds of righteousness because our hearts have changed and because we want to do good deeds. He empowers us by the Holy Spirit to do them. We also do them in obedience, but they don't save us. Ephesians 2:8–9 tells us, "It is by grace that we have been saved through faith, not of ourselves. It is the gift of God, not of works, lest any man should boast" (KJV).

I believe that Paul is talking about positional righteousness here and not deeds of righteousness. It is inextricably interwoven with our faith. When in battle, I will often quote a passage that Paul took from Genesis, and I will say, "I put on the breastplate of righteousness according to the Scripture that says, 'Abraham believed God and it was counted to him for righteousness'" (KJV). In one sense, I think of myself as a frying pan and the enemy's hold over me with past sins and guilt like a handle with which he can control me. I give him the handle and agree with his assessment that I am a sinner and remind him that by faith, I have the righteousness of Christ, thereby removing his right to control me. My good friend says, "When the enemy calls you a dirt bag, agree with him because you were made from the dust of the earth."

The breastplate of righteousness is a piece of armor that protects us from a key weapon of Satan and his demons, called condemnation. Romans 8:1 says, "There is now no condemnation to those that are in Christ" (KJV). We have been forgiven according to the Scriptures, which state in I John 1:9, "If we confess our sins, He is faithful and just to forgive us our sins and to cleanse us form all righteousness" (KJV).

FEET SHOD WITH THE READINESS THAT COMES FROM THE GOSPEL OF PEACE

I love everything about the culture of the outdoor hunting and fishing sports. I love the gear and handmade European guns and the hunting and fishing clothing. As I've said, "Hunting is not a sport; it's a fashion statement." I have wondered if the things that I like to wear are more of an image than a reality of who I am. I've concluded that it's really me. I love good boots, really good boots. My favorite boots are made in Zimbabwe, Africa. An African big-game hunter inspired them. They are considered five-hundred-mile shoes. They were designed for long stalks after dangerous animals, such as elephants, rhinos, cape buffalo, and the big cats. They're made from cape buffalo and impala hide and are incredibly comfortable and durable. The soles resemble truck tire rubber, and they are also very well supported at the ankles.

We are to put on the gospel like a pair of good hunting shoes, but what is the gospel? *Gospel* means "good news." It's defined in I Corinthians 15:3–5: "For what I received, I passed on to you as of first importance, that Christ died for our sins according to the Scriptures, that he was buried, that he was raised on the third day according to the Scriptures, and that he appeared to Peter and then to the twelve" (NIV).

The gospel is the good news of Christ's life, death, burial, resurrection, and ascension to heaven. It's practical good news for you and for me because we can be saved from the stronghold and consequences of sin.

Many booklets have been that describe the matter in four simple points:

1. God loves you and has a plan for your life.
2. Man is sinful. Sin has separated us from God.
3. Jesus Christ is God's provision for our sin.
4. We must individually receive Jesus Christ as our personal savior.

A sinless God became man. He died for our sins so that we could bridge the chasm between a holy God and us. We accept His offering by receiving Him as savior.

I did this on January 1, 1972, in central California. A soldier who I knew from the military base showed up at my doorstep and shared these four simple points with me. I was nineteen years old and had been searching for many years. The Holy Spirit had been convincing, or convicting, me in my conscience that I was a sinner. The Bible says in Romans 3:23, "For all have sinned and fall short of the glory of God" (KJV). I was ready to abandon the last bit of baggage that I was holding onto. What would my friends think? I followed these steps that afternoon and began this journey. Rob, you need to do this if you haven't. It becomes a part of our armor.

The feet imply action. We've got to keep moving and keep telling the story.

There are many effective ways to present the gospel. In the beginning we may only have our story. Then, over the years, we become more sophisticated and educated in the matter. Eventually we end up back at the beginning. We tell our story. "I once was lost, but now I'm found, was blind but now I see." Be prepared to tell your story.

THE SHIELD OF FAITH

Roman warriors had shields that had to be large enough to hide behind. They had to stop flame-dipped arrows, and they could be locked together. Spiritual warfare is a team sport. What if John didn't have a .44 Magnum? What if Edward didn't have a .444 lever-action pointed at the bear? We all need a team of faith-filled men to back us up. Some of the best teams are not your conventional types. They're like these guys. They're the types that you have to lock in cages the night before the battle so that they don't hurt each other. One thing's for sure, though: they'll have your back when the chips are down.

King David, probably the most famous king of all time, understood this. The starting team was a group of very rough men. He was often in very dangerous situations. At a period before he was crowned king, he was in the mountains, fleeing from the current king of Israel, Saul. Saul was very jealous of David for a number of reasons, not the least of which was the close relationship David enjoyed with his son, Jonathan. Saul did not have the respect of his son. David did. I'm sure that it was also because of David's close relationship with the Lord. David had assembled a team of dangerous warriors. First Samuel 22:2 is a description of this motley crew: "All those who were in distress, or in debt or discontented gathered around him, and he became their commander. About four-hundred men were with him" (NIV).

You know my philosophy about mentorship. I have a team of guys who live all over the western United States. They are all proven experts in their given fields. In any new situation that I've found myself, like a new job or church or business, I try to pick up a friend or two with whom I have chemistry. They must be a person bearing good fruit or success in life in an area that I desire to be tutored. There is a certain phenomenon in this important exercise of choosing friends that must be touched on. There is a type of person who has lots of advice and not the kind of visible fruit that qualifies them to become mentors. It is quite epidemic in the area of finance.

One element of their demeanor is pride. This type of person may be the loudest voice, but what does his portfolio look like? One nice thing about business is that the marketplace is self-cleansing, and making money is how you keep score. Good mentors are often unassuming and humble, and it's easy to miss them. Successful men are usually good listeners and have an air of humility about them. They are usually the best students and listeners, and they too love good students. Giving to others is usually a great need in their lives. This is not only true in fiscal matters, but in all areas of life that you wish to emulate. I like to make men like this my coaches and prayer partners. They also share their life's experiences with me to help me along, and I share mine with them. It has become a team of interdependence. You know many of them personally. They wouldn't stand out in a crowd. Your mom and I have trained ourselves to listen to what people do, not just what they say.

NOTE: Success in the marketplace does not automatically qualify you to give spiritual advice. Our culture puts wealthy people on a pedestal. The vocationally successful often feel that it qualifies them to be experts on everything. Even millionaires and billionaires need spiritual advisors. Sometimes qualified mentors are quite middle-class. This is a team sport.

What is faith? Hebrews 11:1 says, "Faith is being sure of what we hope for and certain of what we do not see" (NIV). How do we become sure and certain of things that are unseen, supernatural things? We can grow faith through experiences. We invest our faith with measured risk. Successes will grow our faith.

Contrary to popular belief, however, personal experience is not necessarily the best teacher, and it can have a considerably slower learning curve. At my age, you recognize the need for velocity of money in business and velocity of time in the learning curve. I've found that both can be escalated simply by hanging out with people who have faith and fruit. I prefer to learn from the experiences of others. Proverbs 13:20 says, "He that walks with the wise becomes wise" (NIV). We are today who we will be in many years from now, except for the books that we read and the people who we encounter.

We grow our faith through the books that we read, especially the Bible. The Bible tells us in Romans 10:17, "Faith comes by hearing the message and hearing is heard through the Word of Christ" (NIV). We get to know the author by reading His book. I believe that something supernatural also occurs through a daily systematic reading of God's Word. I've discussed this in greater detail in another letter.

Trials or struggles help us to grow stronger in faith. It builds perseverance, as stated in James 1:2–4.

I think you've got the point. Our faith, and the faith of others and their weapons, is a great shield against the fire-dipped arrows that the enemy shoots at our minds in the form of doubting thoughts and emotions.

The whole black bear experience was such a miraculous event for me, from beginning to end. It could not help but boost my faith. As a matter of fact, at the tail-end of the experience, a particular passage of Scripture was illuminated in my mind. I believe that it was from the Holy Spirit. The backdrop of this passage portrays young David, son of Jesse, giving his resume to King Saul in an attempt to prove his qualifications to have an opportunity to kill the giant, Goliath. David said in I Samuel 17:36–37:

> Your servant has killed both the lion and the bear. This uncircumcised Philistine will be like one of them, because he has defied the armies of the living God. The Lord who delivered me from the paw of the lion and the paw of the bear will deliver me from the hand of this Philistine. (KJV)

This experience with the bear gave me added faith to execute many conquests since then, with the help of my God. By the way, as you know, I did go on to kill a lion also. It was a trophy tom cougar that was killed in Nevada in 2001, in the month of December. This Scripture is handwritten in calligraphy at the feet of the full-standing bear in our living room.

TOM COUGAR
MISSION ACCOMPLISHED

HELMET OF SALVATION

Isaiah describes this as the "helmet of the hope of salvation" in Chapter 59, Verse 17 (NIV). Hope of any kind begins in the mind. I hoped that I'd kill a bear. Thirty years ago, I hoped that your mom would feel about me the way that I felt about her. I have hoped that many things would happen. This hope also deals with the hope of eternal salvation when illuminated by the Holy Spirit. The original languages of the Bible tell us that hope is to anticipate, usually with pleasure or expectation.

The mind is to be protected at all costs. Proverbs 4:3 says, "Above all else, guard your heart, for it is the wellspring of life" (KJV).

The mind is like a sophisticated computer that needs proper programming. People have taken this concept to the extreme. We program our thoughts with what we let into our eye gate and ear gate. Jesus said in Mark 4:24, "Be careful what you are hearing. The measure of thought and study you give to the truth you hear will be the measure of virtue and knowledge that comes back to you" (AMP). Movies, books, the Internet, and the music that we listen to can all shape our thinking.

What we say can program our thoughts. James 3:13 says, "When we put bits in the mouths of horses to obey us, we can turn the whole animal. Or take ships as an example. Although they are so large and driven by strong winds, they are steered by a very small rudder wherever the pilot wants to go. Likewise, the tongue is a small part of the body, but it makes great boasts" (NIV).

Some folks take this to the extreme by thinking that they can steer God's will with their confession. Good luck with that. Others go in entirely the other direction, and that gives them no partnership with God over their future.

When it comes to the battlefield, guard your mind.

THE SWORD OF THE SPIRIT

Use enough gun. We have already touched on this. I was hunting for wild boar last year and was carrying a .357 Magnum pistol. At one time, it was considered the most powerful of handguns. It is pretty powerful and is one of my favorite rounds. There were three wild hogs scurrying down a dirt road toward my friend, Hans, and me. He had a .30-06. I had a 7mm Magnum rifle and a shoulder holstered .357 Magnum. Both long guns are plenty for pigs. He shot the lead pig, a nice black boar of two hundred pounds, and it went right down. I shot the number two pig and blew his shoulder off, but he needed another shot to finish him. In an instant, the number three pig, a smaller boar, went up behind us, and I drew my attention to that one as Hans put number two down. The dogs got the hundred-and-twenty-pound defector cornered, and we followed the dogs in under thick brush, where they cornered him. It took two pistol shots with my .357 Magnum to knock it down and a third in his ear to dispatch it. This last shot was taken with the guide sitting on his back, holding the animal's ears. It's time to upgrade my pistol to a .44 Magnum, .454, or a .500 for wild pigs. A friend of mine had his guide munched on just a few weeks back by a big boar. Use enough gun.

The Bible, when it is used correctly, is like that 444 that sent this big bear to the Promised Land. The Bible says of itself in Hebrews 4:12, "The Word of God is alive and active. Sharper than any double-edged sword and penetrates even to the dividing of soul and spirit, joints and marrow; it judges the thoughts and attitudes of the heart" (NIV).

Jesus set the example of how to execute spiritual warfare in His classic temptation in the wilderness in Matthew, Chapter 4, and Verses 1–11. Go ahead and read it. On the three separate occasions here, He used Scripture as a sword while being tempted. He didn't dialogue or reason with the enemy of our soul. He simply said, "It is written," and quoted appropriate Scripture passages. By the way, Rob, to quote Scripture, you must memorize Scripture. John 3:16 is a great place to start: "For God so loved the world that he gave his only begotten son, that whosoever believeth in him shall not perish, but have everlasting life" (KJV).

The model that I like to use for applying Scripture in battle is James 4:7: "Submit yourself to God, resist the devil and he will flee from you" (KJV). I feel that to properly submit ourselves to God, we must not approach the matter in false Christian bravado. I first accept this concept of embracing my sinfulness and asking forgiveness for any known sin. If you have repented of known sin, you are, in a spiritual sense, dead to sin and alive to God, by faith. It's the same issue discussed in the breastplate of righteousness. After giving the enemy the handle, I then verbally or mentally state a Scripture that refutes the false idea that he's trying to get me to buy into by simply saying, "I rebuke you, Satan, in the name of Jesus, for it is written ..." and I quote an appropriate passage. It may seem a bit corny or religious, but it works. The previous passage says that he will flee from you, and when we are persistent in this discipline, he does go away. Anyway, I hate the sound of crunching bones spiritually and the sight of my own blood.

PRAYING ALWAYS ·

The NIV Bible says, "Be alert and always keep praying for all saints." The King James Version talks about praying "all manner of prayer" in this verse.

We've discussed some details of prayer and how to get answered prayers in another letter. It's worth repeating that thankfulness is a great weapon in prayer. It disarms the enemy and our flesh. It's also worth repeating that we should pray without ceasing in accordance with all of the principles discussed in the letter on prayer.

In closing, let's talk about the big cats. A big mountain lion will grow to two hundred pounds. A big African lion will grow to over five hundred pounds. If an African lion is wounded, he'll hide in the brush and pick out one member of the hunting party to charge. If in that charge, someone doesn't make a kill shot, the targeted human is going to die. The rule of thumb with a leopard is that a wounded leopard will always attack and that every second he is on you translates into twenty stitches.

Robin, Peter said in I Peter 5:8, "Be alert and of sober mind. Your enemy the devil prowls around like a roaring lion looking for someone to devour" (NIV). The King James Version puts it like this: "Be sober, be vigilant: because your adversary the devil, as a roaring lion, walketh about, seeking whom he may devour." Be sure to get really good with these items of protection and with the weapons. It could save your life. It has saved mine. This is the most dangerous game.

Love,

Dad

ORGANIZED RELIGION

> "Let us not give up meeting together, as some are in the habit of doing, but let us encourage one another, and all the more as you see the day approaching." (Hebrews 10:25 NIV)

Dear Robin:

Don't take me too seriously when I say this, but hunting and fishing are like a religion. They have all of the elements of organized religion. There is a social structure, traditions, rituals, cultures, and even texts that we read. The list goes on.

I belong to a few subcultures in the hunting and fishing community. I'd say that you do too, but I won't impose my prejudices on you. You can fish for any kinds of trout that you want.

HUNTING

I admit it. I'm a snob. I'm not saying that it's right, and maybe I shouldn't be so transparent about it, but I know that you know, so there's no hiding it.

I'll try to be careful not to reveal just how bigoted I really am regarding hunting. I see myself as a gentleman sportsman. You might say that when it comes to the accoutrements of the fine sports of wing shooting and big-game hunting, I have champagne taste and a beer budget. The truth is, I'm as much the salt of the earth as the guys who I hunt with. Many of them are just more able to afford the things that I desire, and they are better shots than me.

I love the rich heritage of double-gun wing shooting. You also have been properly instructed that hunting is not a sport; it's a fashion statement. I love fine, handmade European double guns. Anything made in Ferlach, Austria is okay with me. There are no other clothiers than high-end outdoor clothiers. Why own a knife if it doesn't have Sambar stag or ivory handles? They just work better. A belt should be crocodile, and a gun sling should be real horsehair. If your boots aren't made from cape buffalo and impala, they aren't very comfortable. I'm sure you understand that the better the walnut, the better the gun shoots. Teeth and tusks, claws and animal hides in your office are all prerequisites for the sport. Those guys who make accessories like this for suckers like me must be laughing all the way to the bank.

The truth be known, there is a rich history and heritage to all of this. The famous outdoor writers "got it." They created it. I could ramble on and on, but it just makes me want to hunt and fish even more.

When we first started hunting, I wondered where these hunting types congregated. Living in central California, and seeing what some of these agrarian types were driving, I also wondered where they spent their money. I knew that it was here somewhere. I saw it on the symbols on the fronts of their wives' sedans. I also saw it in the size of the tires on their brand-new trucks that had model-number sizes that I didn't even know existed; decals on the rear windows were everywhere.

HUNTING ASSOCIATION DINNER

It started to become clearer to me when we were invited to a dinner for kids. It was a National Hunting Association dinner, and it was held in a dining hall or something. After entering the hall, I saw a big lottery tumbler and men in jeans and cowboy boots with handfuls of hundred dollar bills, buying tickets. We were escorted to our seats, and I looked on the walls. Guns and gear, and guns and gear were everywhere. Did I mention that guns were everywhere? Local sports retailers donated them. I like to think that I'm good with numbers so I did a quick computation. My figures showed somewhere in the quarter of a million dollar range hanging on the walls.

I quickly realized the answer to both of my questions. First of all, the locals spent their hard-earned dough on their kids and their guns. Second, I thought that they all belonged to this particular group until I discovered larger ones.

THE BIG ORGANIZATION

Remember, we're talking about religion here. Here's how it went: I shot this big black bear, as you know. My taxidermist told me that he was an official scorer for them, and he asked if I might want it scored. I told most of this story in another letter, but I didn't tell this part. You have to be a member to get your animal scored, so I joined. It scored very high. He is a gold medal bear, and I was very proud of that.

I had an opportunity to attend the international convention in Reno that year, and I was not prepared for what I saw. There was a convention that covered the size of four football fields, with thousands of people just like me. I had discovered that I belonged to something larger than myself. All of the big gun makers had booths. Every domestic and international outfitter had a booth. For one of the few times that I remember, I felt at home in my own skin and at home in my attire. I discovered a lot more about them and many other organizations. You could do more to preserve the sport and had more opportunity with a large number of members than with "us four and no more."

I found a market for my wildlife art in this show, as well as in other large outdoor expositions and gun shows. I met likeminded people and began to feel that maybe we weren't nuts after all. Maybe we were, but maybe there were other nuts who we could hang out with.

I also discovered that there were a couple of local chapters that I could attend and that they valued guns, hides, wildlife art, and scrimshawed knives as much as I did. I donated some paintings and knives I'd made and discovered that they actually valued my work enough to spend real money for it. At auction, my work commanded surprising prices.

I found a place where I could renew and preserve what I call *the magic.* I could even find new magic there.

CHURCH

Church is sort of like this. It's too easy to say things like, "I was hurt so badly by a church organization that I don't believe in organized religion." As you know, church leaders have thrown me under the bus. Politics exist even in churches. If anyone has a reason to consider themselves a victim of manhandling by Christian leaders, it is I. I have the tire marks on my back to prove it. I still take a strong stand as an advocate for the local church.

I STILL BELIEVE IN THE LOCAL CHURCH

Another common idea is expressed as follows: "I just feel that you don't have to be in a church building. You can be in the church of the great outdoors and that's church."

Besides, you may say, "I feel closer to God there," and, "Organized religion is the reason for most problems among Christians." And the televangelists. Oh, the televangelists.

Sound and balanced theology on this topic contradicts these ideas. It is my opinion that common sense does also.

The church of Jesus Christ has a rich history, heritage, and tradition. My friend, Dr. Bruce Shelley, wrote a comprehensive book entitled *Church History in Plain Language*. Dr. Shelley was senior professor of Church History and Historical Theology at Denver Theological Seminary. He has given me permission to share some of the history of the church as depicted in his book. It's a very scholarly read that is simplified for laymen like you and me. Dr. Shelley and I have had numerous discussions on this and other matters.

Dr. Shelley breaks the past two thousand or so years into a few periods:

6 BC–AD 70	Age of Jesus and the Apostles
AD 70–312	Age of Catholic Christianity
AD 312–590	Age of Christian Roman Empire
AD 590–1517	The Christian Middle Ages
AD 1517–1648	Age of Reformation
AD 1648–1749	Age of Reason and Revival
AD 1749–1914	Age of Progress
AD 1914–Present	Age of Ideologies

Rob, I'll talk about these a little bit, but time will limit me from going into much depth. I heard your sigh of relief.

AGE OF JESUS AND THE APOSTLES: 6 BC—AD 70

It's pretty well accepted that the church was born on the Day of Pentecost in Jerusalem, about two thousand years ago when the Holy Spirit ascended on these new believers. It happened soon after Jesus's ascension, though they were first called Christians in Antioch according to Acts 11:26 (KJV). The early church was initially Jewish, but the dispersal caused by persecution, as well as Paul's missionary work, also spread the culture to non-Jews. They are known as Gentiles.

The early church suffered persecution by the Romans under Nero. Among other things, many were crucified or wrapped in animal skins and fed to large, wild dogs. "Other things" included Nero using Christians as human torches to light his garden.

History tells us that all but one of the original twelve apostles were murdered during this period. Being murdered for the cause of Christ is called *martyrdom*. History says they tried and failed to boil the Apostle John in oil. Paul was also martyred in Rome during this time.

AGE OF CATHOLIC CHRISTIANITY: AD 70—312

The Roman Catholic Church had not yet come into its own. *Catholic* did not have the same meaning that it does today. It meant "undivided and universal."

Christians living in this period were also under persecution from the Romans because they would not partake in emperor worship. The seeds of the Roman Catholic Church were conceived during this time.

The concept of theology, or the systematic study of God's Word, began during the age of Christianity, and heresies were rampant. A famous Greek named Origen reconciled Greek thought with Christian faith, which introduced unification between the educated and cultured people and the simple, but faith-filled, peasants. The New Testament was also compiled and canonized during this time.

AGE OF THE CHRISTIAN ROMAN EMPIRE: AD 312–590

The conversion of the emperor, Constantine, moved Christians from the catacombs to palaces. The center of church government was also moved from Rome to Constantinople. The Roman Catholic Church was established and solidified, as was monasticism. Holy men living in self-imposed poverty and seclusion define monasticism. The concept of the definition of the nature of God was addressed at this time.

AGE OF THE CHRISTIAN MIDDLE AGES: AD 590–1570

Barbarians, floods, and the plague ravaged Rome. Christians attempted to convert others at the end of a holy sword. In Europe, noblemen controlled vast pieces of real estate through feudalism. John Hus and John Wycliff rebelled against Roman Catholicism, stating, "Every man, whether priest or layman, holds an equal place in the eyes of God." The stage was now set for the Protestant Reformation.

AGE OF THE REFORMATION: AD 1517–1648

In the summer of 1520, a document circulated throughout Germany, looking for a man named Martin Luther. It said, "Arise, O Lord, and judge thy cause. A wild boar hath invaded thy vineyard." I have this phrase below a European mounted wild boar's head in my office. It's also engraved on a plaque on a walnut box that I have. My ivory-handled .357 Magnum with bird's-head grips are in the box. I've scrimshawed a wild boar on the grips to celebrate a pig that I shot with it.

Martin Luther strongly resisted the theology of works. The four questions that he addressed were:

1. How is a person saved?
2. Where does religious authority rest?
3. What is a church?
4. What is the essence of Christian living?

The theology stating that we are "saved by faith alone, through grace alone, in Christ alone" was born.

John Calvin emphasized the sovereignty of God, and William Tyndale was murdered. He advocated translating the Bible into the English language. Prior to his martyrdom, he said, "If God spares me before many years pass, I will make it possible for a boy behind the plow to know more Scripture than the clergy."

America was discovered and founded, and this great religious experiment of basing a government solely on God's Word was begun.

Puritans came from Europe for religious freedom with God's Word in one hand and Foxes Book of Martyrs in the other.

Denominationalism was also born as an expression of diversity of orthodox faith.

THE AGE OF REASON AND REVIVAL: AD 1648–1749

The Age of Reason and Revival set reason in the place of faith, and the Renaissance was born. This was the rebirth of classical Greek and Roman culture.

A Great Awakening took place in Europe under men like John Wesley, and it spread to America. There was a movement of mass evangelism in the Colonies under George Wakefield. Reasonable men found common ground with revival men in the birth of the United States of America.

AGE OF PROGRESS: AD 1749–1914

Many things occurred during this age. The French Revolution ushered in Socialism.

The Chapman Sect, which was a small group of Christian businessmen, led to the abolishing of slavery in England. The great missionary movement was born under men like William Carey and Charles Livingstone. A second Great Awakening brought attention to slavery in America, and Protestant Liberalism made Christianity appear more acceptable to the intelligent modern. Liberal theology did and still does challenge the sovereignty of God, the innate depravity of man, Christ's atonement for the forgiveness of sin, the Holy Spirit's role as being essential to conversion, and the eternal separation of the lost to hell.

The Industrial Revolution was born, as well as Friedrich Engel and Karl Marx's introduction of Communism in the publishing of *The Communist Manifesto*. It was rooted in Charles Darwin's humanistic teachings that pervade our current culture. Adam Smith's concept of free market capitalism was challenged, as it is today. The Social Gospel was preached, stating that the primary sin was the capitalist system.

THE AGE OF IDEOLOGIES: AD 1914–PRESENT

Rob, my parents and your mom's parents were born early in this period. World War I occurred and World War II was also fought in this period. Your grandpa, who was ninety years old at the time of the writing of this letter, is a member of the Greatest Generation and fought in World War II. Austrian-born Adolph Hitler led a political movement called Nazism, which glorified a nation and led to the death of millions of Jews, Gypsies, Christians, and other "inferiors." The Russian Revolution also saw millions murdered.

After World War II, great evangelists led millions to Christ in bloodless crusades.

History may be less defined when you are living it, and the importance may seem a bit less significant, but in the mid-1960s, prayer was removed from the public school system. The Vietnam War was occurring, and it was during this time that social unrest gave birth to the flower power generation. "I was there" is not just a statement. I was really there. What was occurring was a perfect storm that just about destroyed a generation of young people. If not for a national revival called the Jesus Movement, we may have suffered even greater losses of our youth. I was very nearly a casualty. Your mom and I accepted Christ in this period.

There were and still are massive revivals in South America, Africa, and other countries, as well as Christian persecutions internationally. A resurgence of political activism among Christians occurred during this time.

I have some pretty strong opinions on the current condition of the church, especially in the West, but I would say that the greatest event that occurred in 2001 is remembered as 9/11. A group of America-hating radical extremists flew jets into a few buildings and killed three thousand people in New York City, Washington, and in Pennsylvania. The jury is still out as to how this part of history will play out, but I will say that it is solely rooted in the theology of radical, militant Islam. I believe that there is nothing greater that we can do to combat this evil than to understand the fundamentals of our faith and to live for Jesus Christ.

That's a very cursory look at the history of the church. I'd like to ask and to answer a couple of questions on the church that are very important.

What is the church and what should take place there?

WORSHIP

The church is the body of all true believers in Jesus Christ. Jesus said that the church is to be a place of worship in Matthew 21:13. The earliest Christians were Jews who met in synagogues and were soon expelled, and then they began to meet in house churches.

FELLOWSHIP

The church is a place of fellowship or *koinonia*. It means "fellowship around spiritual matters." The members of hunting and fishing associations don't fellowship around knitting or scrapbooking. They gather to support and promote a specific cause. Though the church is a place of socialization; it is not a place where our focus should be on business networking or finding a woman, so to speak.

TEACHING AND PREACHING

The church is a place of teaching. The early church devoted themselves to the apostles' teaching, to fellowship, to the breaking of bread, and to prayers (Acts 2:42 NIV).

It is where we are equipped and commissioned for service in our specific area of giftedness, to go out into the marketplace.

SACRAMENTS

The sacraments are the Lord's supper, or Communion, and water baptism.

The Lord's supper is a remembrance of Christ's sacrifice and should be observed as often as possible. We hear the words of Jesus quoted by the Apostle Paul regarding communion as found in I Corinthians 11:23–26:

> For I received of the Lord that which I also passed on to you: The Lord Jesus, on the night that he was betrayed, took bread, and when he had given thanks, he broke it and said, 'This is my body, which is broken for you; do this in remembrance of me'. In the same way, after supper he took the cup, saying, 'This cup is the new covenant in my blood; do this whenever you drink it in remembrance of me. For whenever you eat this bread and drink this cup, you proclaim the Lord's death until he comes. (NIV)

Water baptism is done after conversion in accordance with scriptural example. It is done in obedience as a public testimony to others of your conversion. It represents an invisible and mystical death to sin and resurrection to a new life in Christ (Romans 6:3–4).

GIVING

Financial giving and benevolence should take place there. It should, of course, occur everywhere, but should originate in church. I Corinthians 16:2 instructs us to set aside our donations on the first day of the week for collection.

SPIRITUAL DISCIPLINE

Matthew 18:15–18 gives the formula for spiritual discipline. As a last resort, for the purpose of redemption, a Christian is to be politely and lovingly confronted over in-house matters of sin. It's to be done confidentially by the leadership one-on-one, then with two or more, if necessary, and as a last resort by the membership of the local assembly. In thirty-five years of walking with Christ, I couldn't count on one hand the times that I've seen this become necessary, but it happens. If handled lovingly, professionally, and politely, church discipline can be very effective in salvaging a wayward saint or church body.

ON A PRACTICAL NOTE

It would seem to be acceptable according to Scripture to just meet with a group of friends or with your family regularly and call it church. As Christians, we sometimes get confused between the idea of the church universal, which is all Christians, and the local church assembly. I talked a little about one of my many disappointing experiences with the local church. I have always used Hebrews 10:25, which is our text, to justify the fact that we all needed to be in a local church. I had stated that we are to love the church, warts and all. At a certain point this just wasn't doing it for me alone. I needed a bit more. I was drawn to Acts 20:17–35 and Paul's farewell address to the Ephesians' church that he had founded. This was a local church and was listed among those local churches that Jesus addressed in Revelation, Chapters 2–3. Not long after this I heard something said when a leader asked if there were a country to which we might retreat if America went to pieces. He said, "There is no better place to go. We must stay and fight." It reaffirmed my belief that it is God's plan to use the orthodox local churches, warts and all. It also reaffirmed my belief that it was bad theology to think otherwise. It just doesn't play out well for the long term. Rather than belabor the matter, I'll talk about a recent conversation I had with a friend who told me that he was having difficulties with staying in church. The example should illustrate why church is good for all of us.

He has been a committed Christian for nearly forty years. He has extensive formal Christian education and a national exposure to the Christian community. He had frustrations that were quite warranted, by the way, just as some of mine have been. He knows the Bible as well, or in most cases better, than most pastors of churches. He was having difficulty seeing church as anything more than a spiritual exercise of obedience and a bit of a waste of time. My advice to him was to just find one friend in church who he connected with, who had enough spiritual maturity to stimulate him, and who respected him for his extensive, intimate Christian experience. After that first friend, any further relationships would simply be a bonus. My next suggestion was to make sure that the church that he chose as home had a minister whose messages met his personal needs. I encouraged him that, regardless of his maturity in Christ, we all have needs that can only be met in Christ by another minister's gift. If we can agree that we can't exercise all gifts (only Christ could), then we can be ministered to by their gift.

You'll notice that I used the word *gift* frequently. This is because it is very easy to focus on the value of another's personality or charisma. This is about Jesus Christ and experiencing Him. We can experience hearing Christ by the Holy Spirit through others. We are in need of hearing from others who are mature and who have done their due diligence in areas that compliment ours. If your needs aren't being met fairly regularly from behind the pulpit, find another church.

Do they have room for you? Because my friend is a missionary, he isn't in church every weekend. He really doesn't have time to serve as some would, but the question is, "Does my church offer opportunity to minister in my field of giftedness?"

My point is that we never outgrow challenges, even at very mature levels of spirituality. By overcoming through my failures, I just happened to have a degree of success in this particular area of church attendance. My friend has helped me in many areas. I was honored that he would ask for my thoughts on this matter.

For the newer believer, I'd also ask the following questions:

- Have they consistently upheld essential Christian doctrines?
- Is it a healthy, well-balanced church where God's Word is taught in context?
- Do they affiliate with a denomination or movement where the pastor has a pastor?
- Does it meet my spiritual, social, and emotional needs?

The church has a variety of governmental structures that I wouldn't get too hung up on at first. They are essentially pastoral governed, congregationally governed, and elder run. I personally prefer pastor-run churches where the pastor also has an accountability support structure. It allows for the pastor to promote his vision and be empowered, yet will be held under the accountability of a denomination or movement, as well as a team.

In conclusion, an association can leverage your effectiveness. I know it's a lot of stuff to think about, but I truly believe that, like these hunting (and fishing) associations, we can maximize our efforts by being a part of something bigger than ourselves. In business it's called leverage.

This is very important, whether it be in church attendance or in ministry, so listen very carefully. It is my opinion that it is better to be a small part of something big than a big part of something small. Though we don't want to become part of a lukewarm Christian organization, it has been my experience that lone ranger ministries usually fizzle out either before or after the passing of the founder. I pray that my life's work will outlive me. These types of organizations will often not become a part of a group where complimentary other members of the body of Christ balance their focus. In a best-case scenario, I believe that ministry should be an extension of the local church, which should be connected to a larger governing body. As you know, I have paid a huge price for staying connected to and committed to the local church. I have bus tracks on my back to prove this. I feel that I could easily say that I do not believe in organized religion. Not to appear a victim; I think the saying is true that Christians can be among those that shoot their own wounded. Nevertheless, Christ still died for the church. When it is functioning properly, in the love of Christ, in the supernatural power of the Holy Spirit, and as a well-oiled machine, it is a beauty to behold.

Finishing strong is a huge issue for me. I have been a Christian for many decades. Many that I started with have fully fallen from Christ. Many are living fruitless or limited Christian lives. Some are now in their fifties, sixties, and seventies and are living vibrant Christian lives. I call them thirty- and forty-somethings in Christ. I have walked some over the finish line, and they are in the glorious presence of Christ. The most effective Christians are men and women of the local church.

It was great to chat with you, Rob. Make sure to get your new hunting license. The season is upon us, and the freezer is getting empty.

Love,

Dad

HUNTING BOAR

FIRST BOAR

THE GIFTS THAT COME FROM GOD

"Train up a child in the way he should go (and in keeping with his individual gift or bent), and when he is old he will not depart from it." (Proverbs 22:6 AMP)

September 18, 2007
Dear Robin:

Now, I'm not so foolish as to think that just because you are the son of two Christian parents that you have your ticket to get in. I don't consider the above passage of Scripture to be a promise to Christians and their children. At one time, I did. We have tried our best to give you and your sister the greatest shot at fulfilling this training, flawed as we are. Now that I've been at this for a while, I have come to believe that God doesn't have any grandkids. There seems to be this pesky matter of free will that is involved. I now believe that if you do decide to walk with Christ for a lifetime, it is completely up to you.

I do feel that it has been our responsibility to find something that our children are good at and to help them excel in it. Our text passage supports this idea.

I chose this passage for an entirely different reason than is most often coined in Christian circles. I selected it for the purpose of discussing gifts and temperaments. I also quote this verse from the Amplified Bible because I feel that it best describes the idea.

We discovered a long time ago that you are a good angler and a great shot. You are very intuitive at all things that occur in the wild. Given the incredible list of choices in outdoor sports, I think that it may be unrealistic to believe that we can be good at all of them. We can discover what we like and what we don't like. For example, I don't hate bass fishing, but I love trout fishing. I don't hate turkey hunting, but I adore wild boar hunting. I think that you get the point.

THE RANCH

FIRST TROUT

FIRST PHEASANT

About June of 2003, we met a rancher named Sal. We were working our German shorthaired pointer named Buster with our dog trainers, Bob and Janice, in an alfalfa field that they had secured for training. While working this magnificent, bright-white specimen of a bird machine, Sal, who was standing at the edge of the field, approached us and offered us an opportunity to do two things. He said that we could work with Buster on his twenty-eight-hundred-acre grape ranch in Hickman that had gone to seed. He also said that we could shoot any rabbits or other game that we encountered. We signed up immediately. Much to our pleasant surprise, this was the beginning of one of the greatest adventures of our hunting career. These sorts of things don't come along too often, and we took full advantage of it.

Not long after this encounter with Sal, we visited this ranch of hills with rows of grape vine after grape vine after grape vine. We introduced ourselves to Francois, the caretaker, with gift in hand of fish and wild game, along with the golden ticket: Sal's name. Francois instructed us on the drill. He told us what dirt roads to take and where the boundary lines were. The place was a veritable rabbit factory. We saw dozens of jackrabbits and cottontails in the perfect habitat. They hid in foot-high grass and scurried across roads. They hid in piles of brush. They stood in plain view. There were pigeons and doves and signs of coyotes (though we never got one of them), and we had it all ... to ... ourselves. The dream lasted two and one-half years. After this period, the ranch changed hands, and the new owners forbade any hunting. Someone had vandalized some equipment, and they had to shut us down. In that time, we had honed our skills on every imaginable caliber of pistol and rifle. We used many gauges of shotguns, and we ate rabbits, lots of rabbits. We never brought ourselves to eat the jackrabbits. Killing without eating was, of course, justified by the fact that this was a hunt designed to eliminate varmints. We do eat pretty much everything that we harvest, including the occasional rattlesnake. Did you notice that I used the word *harvest* for *kill* because it is more politically correct? After all, this is California. Fortunately, we have friends who love cottontail rabbits, because eating rabbits got old.

Our journals tell of you getting so adept with a 22-caliber single-shot rifle that you could hit a jackrabbit at 150 yards, in the eye. We shot pigeons with a .410 shotgun, a 20-gauge, and a 12-gauge. We shot .357 Magnum pistols, .22 pistols, .380 autos, .243 and .45-70-caliber rifles and more. We discovered what we liked and didn't like about each of them. We also brought friends and trained young men and discovered what we did and didn't like about them.

OWLS

I'm sure you remember the time that we were hunting with your longtime friend. I have a photo of you and Herbie standing behind a row of eleven cottontails on the ground. We cleaned them well beyond dark by the light of the headlights on my Toyota truck. Your assignment was to help me clean the bunnies. Herbie's job was to ward off owls that were swooping down to steal our treasure.

As I said, the dream did finally come to an end, as we suspected that it might, but not before we both became pretty darned good hunters. It is wonderful to note that we were able to spend the final trip with our good friend, Wayne. I'm so glad that I could share it with him and with you.

FRESNO COUNTY

Just as there are a multitude of different types of hunting and fishing, there is also a huge array of our spiritual and vocational gift options. I wanted to talk a bit about these matters in two categories and touch on what I feel are some vital issues.

Now, addressing these topics in the context of essentials is a bit dicey because neither of them is necessarily nonnegotiable in the purest ideological sense. What I mean by that is vocational gifts and spiritual gifts fall more under the category of educated opinions rather than strict truths in a biblical context. Bible teachers have debated over the definitions of *spiritual gifts* for centuries. On the subject of vocations, it is probably an even more broadly debated subject. It can be subjective as to how to define them and how to find your calling.

First of all, I'm going to offer some tools that have been helpful to your mom and me in defining and discovering vocational gifts. Second, we'll discuss what I feel is a good biblical model for spiritual gifts. It is, in my view, a good approach that has helped me to be effective in understanding my own place in this life.

VOCATIONAL GIFTS

Before investigating some ideas about vocational calling, or how we make money, let me say that some people make their money to feed their family through their ministry. Some people, like me, are called to the marketplace. We are often called "laymen," though the spiritual responsibilities are no less for mature Christians than they are for ministers. The Puritans are quoted as saying that they believed that every man had a calling. They said, "If you be a man without a calling, having no calling tending to public good, yet have two-thousand to spend, thou art as an unclean beast." We are all ministers by biblical definition (I Peter 2:9).

It is worth noting that Paul was a tentmaker by trade and an apostle by ministry calling. This is found in Acts 18:3

TEMPERAMENT

Let's talk about temperament. The passage that we opened with implies that we all have different gifts and bents. That would be our temperament, or how we are wired.

There is some ancient Greek thinking on this topic that I believe offers a tremendous tool to understand ourselves. You and I are very different in temperament. Just as you shoot a .243 for long-range shots on big game, I prefer a 7mm Magnum. Just as you prefer pump shotguns, I prefer doubles.

Many respected ministers have adopted a model to help us with our understanding of temperament. Simply stated, they write that people will fall into one, or a unique combination, of four temperaments.

- ✦ The Party Person
- ✦ The Peacemaker
- ✦ The Worker/Leader
- ✦ The Contemplative Perfectionist

A one-paragraph definition of this multifaceted subject is not really enough to help you understand this concept. You must read up on this. There are several popular books. It is enough, however, to help you to see why we are all so different. Paul asks us the question in I Corinthians 4:7,

"Who maketh thee to differ one from another?" (KJV). The answer, of course, is that God does. Reading the book and taking the test in the book is, in my opinion, a must-do for every serious vocation-seeking Christian.

THE LADDER OF VERTICAL ALIGNMENT

In discovering and implementing our spiritual and vocational gifts, your mom and I have adopted a philosophy that we coined "the ladder of vertical alignment" (KJV). Jesus was asked what the greatest commandment was. His answer is found in Matthew 22:36–39. Quoting from Leviticus 19:18, Jesus told those who questioned Him that the first and greatest commandment was to love the Lord thy God with all of thy heart, soul, mind, and strength, and that the second was like unto it. It was to love your neighbor as yourself. To filter decisions about career and ministry through this priority ladder brings a lot of long-term balance to our lives.

If, in our choices, we can place God first, our spouse second, our family third, our career and ministry fourth, and ourselves as last, we can dodge the bullet of imbalance. Many men place their career first, and the other priorities in their lives in various order of priority. I chose to adopt my dad's strengths and reject his weaknesses. It is common for men to place their careers first. It is said that men get their self-esteem and identity from their work. I saw a bumper sticker recently that read: "God first, family second, and country third." A well-meaning Christian missed a very important point. We are to put God first, *our spouse* second, then family and country. We can't allow ourselves to forget date night.

Another misconception many women have is that if they are placing their children first, that they are putting their family in proper priority alignment. This is also common due to maternal instincts. Please don't hear what I'm not saying. Every category gets out of balance for seasons, and sometimes this is good. For example, a mother with young children must devote an apparently unbalanced amount of time and energy to the raising of the children. In the launching stages of business endeavors, men often need to spend extra hours.

Another misconception that many in public ministry have is that if they are putting their ministry first, they are putting God's work first and therefore putting God first. What I'm saying is that God is first and foremost in my life, your mom is my first ministry, you kids are my second, and the community comes in last.

It is interesting to note that in our culture, we so idolize financial success that we ignore the obvious regarding other important priorities. Sometimes a truly balanced person is viewed as mediocre when, in fact, they may be quite successful by biblical definition. I'm not endorsing laziness, but I think that you get the idea.

The point is that if we know what any financial vehicle is and is not designed for, we will not try to get it to do something that it's not designed to do. For example, a job will almost never create passive income. That's just the way it is. A job can, however, meet our daily needs.

FREE-ENTERPRISE CAPITALISM

We enjoy an economic system in the United States that allows the most opportunity to prosper financially because it is built upon God's Word. Ask anyone from a foreign country who owns a business in the States. Our financial system is called free-enterprise capitalism. It's founded upon the idea that our material success occurs from natural resources leveraged through our efforts with private ownership of tools. When the tools of production are owned by people in the private sector and not by the government, people are much more motivated to produce.

Governor William Bradford introduced a form of free-enterprise capitalism to the Pilgrims in the early 1600s. Their first year on Western soil was a disaster. They were operating under a form of collectivism, imposed on them by the English. More than half of them died, and thirty-year-old William Bradford instituted a form of capitalism. He gave them each a plot of land, and they were to live on what each produced, not the equal distribution of all. They could then sell any excess. They never starved again.

A theologian named Adam Smith defined free-market capitalism in the formative stages of our country. It is a biblical study of economics that defines our current fiscal system. We are the wealthiest nation that has ever existed because of our economic system. On the flip side, Cuba, a forty-year experiment in Communism, is a dismal failure. A reporter recently visited Cuba and noted that he did not see a vehicle on the streets any newer than a 1959 model. The average citizen makes ten dollars per month. Doctors do much better. They make twenty dollars. The opposite of Capitalism is Socialism and, in its extreme sense, Communism. The government owns the tools of production in pure Socialism.

I also choose to not assign spiritual value to wealth. Money itself is neither good nor evil. What men do with money makes it good or evil. It's like guns. Some say that guns kill people. The obvious response to that is that guns do not kill people; people with guns kill people. My friend says that wealth doesn't ruin people. It reveals and amplifies their true character. Were they greedy before having wealth? It reveals and amplifies it. Were they generous, responsible, and frugal? It does the same.

TAKING THE SHOT ON A 365 LB BLACK BEAR WITH A 45–70 IN CALAVARAS COUNTY, CA., NOV. 2004

BUDGETING

The rules of business and budgeting are simple. We have to have as much coming in as there is going out. Whatever is left is called profit. This is as true in principle for a high school senior as it is for a multimillion dollar business. If you come up short, you can do one or both of the following: You can make more or spend less. You line out your personal budget by determining all expenses and compare it against after-tax income. This is the nut that you must crack, in business vernacular.

Our family budget has served me well for many years. There are extra lines for extra line item budget expenses and spaces to have precise amounts placed on a weekly schedule. At the top is a weekly tracking mechanism. There are many sample budgets that are available. One of the great pleasures that I take in life is to highlight bills paid with a yellow pen. It doesn't take much to please me, I guess.

By the way, time management is time budgeting. I've been accused of being good at time and money management. The truth be known, I'm lazy. The more efficiently I can get my work done, the more time I have to hunt and fish. It has been insinuated by some that I'm cheap. I'm not cheap; I'm frugal. The more I have left over, the more I have for guns and trips, and the more your mom has for toys also. Regarding my toys and spoken like a true statesman, my good friend and professional hunter says, "Life is too short to shoot an ugly gun."

DEBT

Debt elimination will create freedom. The following is how to eliminate debt:

1. Create an emergency fund.
2. Pay off all debt, beginning with the smallest and then moving to the largest ones.
3. Create a cushion equaling three to six months of income.
4. When steps one through three are completed, move into investments.

This is a very simplified explanation of the strategy.

GIVING

Giving is a vital discipline to the Christian life. The common response to giving is that we promise to give when we can afford it or, "If I win the lottery, I'll give a million dollars to my church." My good friend and successful business owner says, "If you don't give out of a little, you won't give out of a lot." It all sounds very cliché, but Jesus made it quite clear in Luke 6:38 that if we give, it will be given back to us, pressed down, shaken together, and running over (KJV). It's important to note that God is not a slot machine. You don't put the money in this side and expect a return on investment to spit out the bottom. He does give back, but it's not out of obligation and it isn't always monetary. He gives because He's good and it's good for us to give.

Unfortunately, many outdoorsmen adopt the view that if we stop going to church, we get a 10 percent raise and the day off to go fishing or hunting.

TITHING

I don't wish to belabor the subject of tithing as an Old Testament law that we need not adhere to. I call 10 percent a good start. If we fall back in our giving, which I have at times, we can incrementally work our way back to a 10 percent minimum at a small percentage increase per month. This is just a suggestion that has worked for us. I've never seen a businessperson who gives generously be disappointed in his personal prosperity. On the other hand, I've never seen a businessperson who isn't giving generously become financially blessed. I've not seen them experience miraculous circumstances and be prosperous for a sustained period.

We give out of obedience, love for God, and love for the needs of others. Your mom and I are afraid not to give at this point. It's a line item expense.

SPIRITUAL GIFTS

Rob, just as every species that we hunt or fish has characteristics that are specific to them, so do we. The Bible tells us in Psalms 139:14 that we are fearfully and wonderfully made (KJV). God has created us and endowed us with specific gifts. Your gifts are different than mine. They are a unique combination of what God has bestowed specifically on you.

Paul characterized the greater group of believers like a body with individual parts. It's commonly referred to as the body of Christ in Romans, Chapter 12. We are individual members of the body that work together to make a whole, like the different body parts that make up a complete body.

There is much controversy over this topic of spiritual gifts. I will try to simplify it as best I can. First of all, as I stated previously, the topic is a nonessential by definition. It is my view that those who speak definitively about something that God's Word does not can easily get into trouble. On the topic of nonessentials, C.S. Lewis said, "One of the things Christians disagree about is the importance of their disagreements. When two Christians of different denominations start arguing, it is usually not long before one asks whether such-and-such a point really matters and the other replies: Matter? Why, it's absolutely essential." This is certainly true of spiritual gifts.

GIFTS OF MINISTRY

Many have said that certain gifts have passed away with the apostles, and others lump gifts of the Spirit in with ministry gifts. To add further confusion, these, as well as many other views, are acceptable. For the sake of simplicity on a not-so-simple topic, if it is in the Bible and if it is not stated clearly that certain gifts have passed away, I accept them as in use today. I accept many other views on this as orthodox and simply disagree all or in part, and would ask the same courtesy of my brothers and sisters in Christ. It's important that we agree on the essentials listed in our first letter, not on nonessentials such as these.

I will try to portray what I feel is a common-sense view of spiritual gifts as I see them in context with all Scripture. I would also say that I don't feel confused about my own spiritual gifts. I'll tell you what I do know and not pretend to know what I do not know.

There are a number of lists of gifts in the New Testament and some gifts referred to in the Old Testament as well. I'll give a few references here shortly.

It appears that there are two categories of spiritual gifts. They are gifts of the Holy Spirit and vocational gifts of ministry.

VOCATIONAL GIFTS OF MINISTRY

These are spiritual callings of ministry that are much like spiritual vocations or offices. They are permanent, spiritual offices that God gives to each of us and they have defined titles and job descriptions. It is like the idea that we are on a job search and discover that we are best suited to become a plumber. In our career search, we eventually find what is called a *fit* in common vernacular. This does not mean that we are now a plumber and can start plumbing. We must go to plumbing school or enter an apprentice program, or we will forever be amateurs. For example, do you want an untrained surgeon adlibbing through your abdomen?

The lists that assign these gifts are found in Romans 12:1–8, I Corinthians 12 (excluding verses 8–10), and Ephesians 4:7–13. I'll also discuss I Corinthians, Chapter 14 soon.

There is a shorter list of some vocations found Ephesians 4:7-13. These gifts are often referred to as "the fivefold ministries" because there are five of them. They are: Apostle, Prophet, Evangelist, Pastor, and Teacher.

Let's take the vocational gift of evangelist listed here in Ephesians as an example. The Greek tells us that an evangelist is a preacher of the gospel. You may know people like this. That is all they can think about and talk about. A good example of an evangelist is Phillip, the evangelist found in Acts 8:27-39. He is also called an evangelist in Acts 21:8. Most titles and examples are not necessarily explained as clearly as this one is in Scripture, but a little digging and studying can reveal a lot.

GIFTS OF THE HOLY SPIRIT

The reason that I call them the gifts of the Holy Spirit is because the Bible does. In my view, these are not permanent, vocational ministry gifts. They are distributed by the Holy Spirit, as needed for specific circumstances and in specific instances.

There are nine gifts of the Holy Spirit listed in I Corinthians 12:8–10. They are:

+ The Word of Wisdom
+ The Word of Knowledge

+ The Gift of Faith (not to be confused with the measure of faith that we have all been given) (Romans 12:3 KJV)
+ Gifts of Healing
+ Working of Miracles
+ Prophecy
+ Discerning (or distinguishing between) Spirits
+ Tongues
+ Interpretation of Tongues

I feel that an in depth study of both sets of gifts would not be appropriate in the context of these letters. It could take a whole book to explain them. I do hope to address this someday soon in a more comprehensive text.

Jesus was used in all of these gifts, other than tongues and interpretation of tongues, as best as I can tell. Now this brings us to what may be the most controversial of topics: the gift of tongues.

THE GIFT OF TONGUES

This is what I do know:

The gift of tongues is listed among the other eight gifts of the Holy Spirit in I Corinthians 12:10.

Paul did ask the question, "Do all speak with tongues?" in I Corinthians 12:30. This seems to imply that all do not speak with tongues. I would, of course, agree. All do not have the gift of tongues that would be followed by an interpretation of tongues, but all can pray in tongues for a private devotion.

Here are a few instances where this gift or baptism in the Holy Spirit, as some call it, was given. See Acts 2:1–4, Acts 10:44–46, and Acts 19:1–8.

The interpretations of this experience vary widely. Some believe that you are baptized in the Holy Spirit at conversion. Others see it as a separate experience. Both views are acceptable. I would, however, object to the idea that you must pray in tongues to be saved. This is a contradiction to the principles of salvation by grace alone, through faith alone in Christ alone as portrayed in Ephesians 2:8–9.

Some believe that we can all speak in tongues. I believe this. Paul tells us in Romans 8:26 that the Holy Spirit helps us in our weaknesses with groans that cannot be expressed. I believe this is praying in tongues. In I Corinthians 14:21 he quoted from Isaiah 28:11–12 regarding these strange tongues, is the rest that causes the weary to rest. Others believe that it is a gift of the Holy Spirit that is distributed by Him and is not for all believers. I believe this Scripture reveals both are true. One is for private use in our prayer closet in a private prayer language, and the other is for use in public church assembly as tongues alongside another gift of interpretation of tongues expressed much like prophecy.

Chuck Smith said:

> We believe that there is an experience of empowering of the Holy Spirit in the life of the believer that is separate and distinct from the indwelling of the Spirit that takes place at conversion. Jesus made three promises to us about the Spirit. He is with you (before conversion). He shall be in you (after conversion), and you shall receive the power when He comes over you or upon you. This coming upon you has been referred to as the baptism of the Holy Spirit or overflow of the Spirit.

Robin, in this context, the "coming over you" is to equip you for service as well as for personal edification or "building up with" a private "prayer language."

The founder of a very successful drug rehabilitation program was asked to explain the students' miraculous success rate in overcoming these devastating addictions. After interviewing several students, the unanimous conclusion echoed was: "the baptism in the Holy Spirit." Salvation provided redemption, and the baptism in the Holy Spirit provided the power to overcome and then thrive.

It is once again my opinion that this apparent contradiction is resolved by reading the entire fourteenth chapter of I Corinthians in context.

The gift of tongues that Paul discussed in I Corinthians 12:30 is described as being exercised in public only with an interpretation. It is for the edification of the church. Otherwise, praying in an unknown tongue for personal edification is to be exercised in the privacy of your prayer closet.

The subject is in and of itself a nonessential and with varying views. I would discuss this subject with other believers, but would not divide over it. This seems to be a fair observance of the subject.

By the way, I would not categorize any spiritual gifts as a badge of spirituality. The Corinthian church "came behind in no spiritual gift," but were grossly immature spiritually. This is found in I Corinthians 1:7. Many of my non-charismatic or non-Pentecostal brothers and sisters live far more balanced lives than some of my charismatic and Pentecostal friends. Unfortunately, many who seem to be sensitive to spiritual things feel that they have a corner on the market of spiritual gifts and are just waiting for the others to come around. I emphasize that this is spiritual arrogance and would remind them that along with Paul, "I pray in tongues more than you all" (KJV). I'm saying this to make a point. This arrogance can alienate the sincere and can drive people away from a wonderful experience.

These gifts are simply tools for equipping and empowering us to do God's work.

Robin, though there is much controversy on the topic, as your dad, I did feel compelled to give my views on the subject.

Well, I know that this is a lot of stuff to digest. I appreciate your willingness to look it over. I was so pleased that when I presented the first draft of these letters to you on your eighteenth birthday, you insisted on keeping the copy rather than having me hold onto them for you. This made me feel that you valued them.

I experienced something that had a significant effect on me when your grandfather was living. Because he lived with us for the last fifteen years of his life, we saw his very gradual, physical deterioration firsthand. The only way I know to describe it was that it was like watching that graphic that we've all seen of man as he supposedly evolved and began to walk upright. We watched it in reverse as he emerged daily from his bedroom. He would walk to the kitchen table, and your mom would serve him coffee. At seventy-five years old, he was lifting free weights. By his late eighties, he was bent over, barely walking, and had difficulty lifting the coffee cup to his lips. In about the last year of his life, he was in a wheelchair, unable to feed himself and in a residential care home. He left a great legacy of devoting the last years of his life to Christ, to us, and also his service as a World War II hero.

This caused me to do some serious soul-searching. I came to realize and embrace the importance of leaving a legacy for you; your sister, Lindsay;

and possibly others. The Bible tells us that we all have a race to run, a cross to bear, and a field in which we should look for our treasure. In this great country, we also have the ability to live under our own vine and fig tree. Our legacy may not be as great as some, but if we are faithful in becoming the best that we can with what God has given us, it should be greater than our parents. I pray that you will build on the good that your mom and I leave behind and filter out the bad.

I hope that these letters will help you in the years to come. I'm proud to call you my son and to have you as my namesake. I think that it's just about time for us to go out and *harvest* something.

Love,

Dad

YOU CALLED THEM ISH.

ABOUT THE AUTHOR

Robin Wood was born in upstate New York, attended art school at one of the most prestigious schools in Boston, and attended Bible University in central California. He holds numerous world records and outdoor awards with virtually all of the best-known hunting and fishing organizations in the world. Living in northern California, he is a volunteer teacher of the Bible at Sacramento Teen Challenge.

Printed in the United States
By Bookmasters